Seizing
the ASI Spirit

Kenneth Livesay

HART RESEARCH CENTER
FALLBROOK, CALIFORNIA

Edited by Ken McFarland
Cover art direction and design by Ed Guthero

The author assumes full responsibility for the accuracy of all facts, quotations, and references as cited in this book.

ISBN 1-878046-32-2

Dedication

To my dear wife, Ruth Marie Walter-Livesay.

This book could not have been written without Ruth's support and her skills in editing and composition. Ruth has been a great wife and companion for over fifty-one years and a great support during our forty years in the ministry.

I appreciate her deep interest in Adventist-Laymen's Services and Industries, reflected in the many hours she has spent in helping to complete this book.

Contents

About the Author

One day while working at the ASI office at the General Conference, I received about fifty applications for ASI membership. Never had so many applications from one conference been received in the ASI office at one time. They were from Elder Kenneth H. Livesay, ASI secretary for the Southeastern California Conference. ASI was obviously on the move in Southeastern California! Needless to say, it made quite an impression on me and made me want to meet the person who had sent in this huge stack of applications.

At the next national convention in Galveston, Texas, while registering the attendees, I met this dynamic and friendly leader. Then in 1981, when Ken became the newly elected executive secretary and treasurer of ASI, I began to work with him.

As I became acquainted with Ken, I learned that he had graduated from Broadview Academy in Illinois and then served in the United States Army during World War II. Afterward, he earned a Bachelor of Arts degree from Emmanuel Missionary College in 1952 and a Master of Arts degree from Andrews University in 1960.

The Livesays began their ministry in Cheboygan, Michigan, in 1952. In 1955, they moved to the Chesapeake Conference, where Ken pastored the Wilmington, Delaware, and then Spencerville, Maryland, churches. Then in 1960, the Livesays moved to California, where Ken served as chaplain for the Paradise Valley Hospital and later as pastor of the El Cajon Church. From there they went to the Southeastern California Conference office, where he served as the director of Personal Ministries and as the ASI secretary until he came to the General Conference. Thus he brought with him many years of experience in personal witnessing.

While working in the Southeastern California Conference, Elder Livesay helped initiate "SDA Laymen's New Church Development, Inc." He worked with this group to develop "ASI Mission Church Builders"—a volunteer program in the Pacific Union Conference for helping build new churches.

As ASI secretary, he visited each ASI member in his conference every year to encourage, exchange ideas, and become better acquainted. Membership grew rapidly because of Ken's active pursuit of qualified professional and business people in the conference.

For several years Ken was chosen by the ASI National Program Committee to be the coordinator for the Witnessing Program at the national ASI conventions because of his vivacious spirit and love of personal, Christ-like witnessing. Many times he has stated his conviction that the mission of ASI is to share, support, and inspire—and to stimulate members for outreach in their local churches and conferences. Ken believes ASI Christians can best accomplish this mission when they sense God's presence in their lives and are confident that the Spirit will speak through them.

When asked by a conference official what was being done for the local church member at ASI meetings, he answered, "We set them on fire for God, and when they return home they will be the best missionaries in your churches, because the ASI objective is to share the good news in the marketplace in such a positive and loving manner that people will respond to the love of Christ."

At the national ASI office at the General Conference, I

found Ken Livesay to possess a salesman's personality—he is a salesman for Christ! In working with him, I learned that he made strategic plans and chose people with the right skills to do a job, then allowed them to do their best for the total program in order to give honor to God.

Ken has never been one to leave details to the last moment, so he never looked or acted hurried, yet each day he accomplished much. He practiced good business management with the Lord's money, as he did with his own. And he always practiced the "Golden Rule."

Back in academy, Ken had to work hard because he needed to earn all of his way through school. In fact, during that time he would go to church and not take off his coat, because his one Sabbath shirt was torn down the back! Perhaps this is why he is able to relate especially well, not just to those whose businesses are large and successful, but to those operating small, struggling ones. Regardless of the size of the business or institution, he treats each member with the same respect.

One day he told me that he tries to live by a verse underlined in his mother's Bible: "He has showed you, O man, what is good, and what does the Lord require of you? To act justly, to love mercy and to walk humbly with your God." Micah 6:8, NIV.

—Julia W. Norcott

Foreword

Questions about the ASI organization and its relation to the Adventist church seem to come up on a fairly regular basis. In fact, strange as it may seem, this organization, established back in 1947, is still relatively unknown by many of our Adventist church members. Since I have had the opportunity of working closely with the ASI and its leaders, I am optimistic that this book can make a real contribution in spreading the word about the positive impact ASI is making in its support of the organized Seventh-day Adventist church.

With his many years of experience as a leader in ASI, Elder Kenneth Livesay is certainly well qualified to write this important work. It is his intention that readers will become better acquainted with the mission and activities of ASI.

Adventist laymen—and particularly those in business and professional vocations—have the opportunity of influencing the world for good in ways that the organized church could never do. Adventist-Laymen's Services and Industries has recognized this responsibility. Its motto, "Sharing Christ in the Marketplace," has had a profound impact on many communities. The decade of the 90s has seen increased activity by the laity of the church in many positive roles.

Everywhere you look, ASI is making an impact on the North American Division—and even the world field—for great good. Only the Lord knows the total result for good as He sees the influence of these entrepreneurs in business and in witnessing.

I certainly wholeheartedly support the efforts of Elder Livesay as he tells the ASI story, and I am sure this book will heighten awareness of the opportunities available to potential ASI members.

As you read these pages, a picture will emerge of dedicated men and women seeking to utilize their talents for the advancement of God's cause. It was this organization that coined the term "Supporting Ministries" to communicate to the church that, though they are not supported with church funds, they are working in harmony with the mission and ministry of our church.

As we look ahead, I am sure the 90s will see an expanding role for the laity in our church. In the event that you qualify for ASI membership, I urge you seriously to consider becoming a member of this vibrant organization.

Robert S. Folkenberg
President
General Conference of Seventh-day Adventists

Acknowledgments

For several years, ASI members have urged me to write a book about our organization. Julia Norcott, my former secretary at the General Conference, often asked me—both before and since my retirement—when I was going to write the book. I began writing in earnest after her phone call in June of 1992.

Madlyn Hamblin encouraged me long before my retirement to write a book about ASI. She gave me a copy of the book, *If I Can Write, You Can Write*, by Charlie Shedd. Madlyn wrote on the flyleaf, "You must write a book. This volume of excellent 'tips' will help you get started. Sincerely, Madlyn Hamblin."

I am indebted to many others, especially the officers and pioneers of ASI. Credit must be given to Dr. E.A. Sutherland, who blazed the trail in both Christian education and the lay movement in the church. Dr. Sutherland really started ASI.

Acknowledgments are also in order for the contributions of all former and current officers of ASI. Dr. Sutherland was the first president, followed by Dr. L.A. Senseman, Allan Buller, Roger Goodge, Harold Lance, Philip Winsted, Henry Martin, and Ray Hamblin. Dr. Wayne McFarland was the first executive secretary-treasurer, followed by Elder Wesley Amundson, Elder Caris Lauda, Elder James Aitken, myself, Elder Conn Arnold, and Elder Ed Reid.

Along with these leaders, the writings of several church pioneers supplied me with valuable information used in this book. Other sources of documentation came from many articles in the *ASI News* and from former students of Madison College. Such men as Roger Goodge and Elder Leland Straw worked closely with Dr. Sutherland for years, and they supplied first-hand information about the beginnings of ASI. I also thank Robert Zollinger for the information he supplied for the chapter on the Laymen's Foundation.

I salute ASI members for their dedication to a finished work.

Introduction

Many in the Adventist church know little about the ministry and mission of Adventist-Laymen's Services and Industries (ASI). I find it interesting to discover how some Adventists perceive the organization.

Recently I asked a professional man, "What comes to your mind when you hear the acronym ASI?" He thought for a moment and said, "I think about some rich Adventists—a bunch of do-gooders with their money." A building contractor said, "I can't take time now to go build churches."

In spite of all the good publicity ASI is receiving, those of us associated with it need to communicate what our primary mission is. We need to make known to our church that we are lay missionaries who support ourselves by our business or profession.

This book is divided into four sections. The first describes how and why ASI was started and shares how meaningful the conventions are to those who attend. Section two reveals the missionary spirit and witnessing experiences of several ASI members. Section three records the rich heritage of six institutions and their Christian work. Section four has a chapter about the future plans of ASI and concludes with a chapter inviting qualified Adventists to join the ASI organization. Obviously, one book cannot cover all ASI members or institutions. But included here are the stories of some who are representative of the many dedicated laymen who daily demonstrate a happy, positive, Christian spirit in the marketplace and in their churches. This book strives not just to present a report of what ASI members are doing in witnessing and outreach. Its wider purpose is to help readers catch the very spirit of Adventist families who belong to ASI.

The *Adventist Review* has done a great service in sending its editors to ASI national conventions for several years. Their coverage has been excellent. Still, when we talk to potential members, we sense that the mission of ASI is not clearly understood. The dedicated Adventist family that belongs to ASI is a tremendous asset to the local church and conference. For it is in the local church, conference, and community that ASI members are most active and effective.

I have served as an ASI secretary on the local conference level and at the General Conference for twenty-three years, including seven years as an honorary member since retirement. It is impossible for me fully to describe the impact of ASI on my life. It remains my purpose to do what I can to influence business and professional members in the Adventist church seriously to consider membership in this positive Christian organization. Something happens to laymen when they catch the spirit and dynamics of ASI.

Membership in ASI at this writing has increased to over 1,000 in the North American Division. Over the last twenty years, attendance at the national conventions has grown tremendously. At the first national convention I attended in 1971, held in San Diego, California, there were about thirty-five in attendance. There were 1,534 in attendance at the 1992 convention in Palm Springs.

In 1983, the British Union invited the officers of the national ASI to help organize the first overseas chapter. Since then, several divisions—including the Far Eastern, South American, and European Divisions—have formed ASI chapters.

Why is ASI growth soaring? Business and professional

members are experiencing inspiration and dynamic personal Christian growth through their association with ASI. The convention programs are planned to meet the personal and professional needs of each member. And when business and professional families hear their fellow members describe how they have witnessed and shared the gospel in the marketplace, they want to become involved too. They catch a vision of how the power of the Holy Spirit can work through them to share Christ with people in the business community.

1

Why Did It Take So Long?

It was one of those wonderful, pleasant Sabbath mornings in the San Diego, California, area back in 1961. Our family went to Sabbath School and worship services as usual. Little did I realize that what I was to hear that morning would profoundly affect my future ministry.

Our pastor introduced Elder Wesley Amundson, executive secretary-treasurer of the Association of Privately Owned Institutions and Businesses from the General Conference of Seventh-day Adventists. I do not remember if he used a Bible verse for his message. I cannot recall much of what he said, except for the fact that he talked about laypersons being involved in personal evangelism in their work.

Elder Amundson talked about the mission of ASI with great enthusiasm and excitement. He shared stories of many people—employees, customers, and others—who had become Christians as a result of the outreach activities of ASI men and women. It may have been his emphasis on lay evangelism that captured my attention. I had been a pastor for ten years, and this was the first time I had heard anything about ASI. Now the seed was planted in my mind, and I was curious.

At the time, I was serving as a chaplain in the Paradise Valley Hospital. The following Monday morning at the hospital, I commented to one of our employees about the Sabbath morning sermon.

"Have you ever attended an ASI convention?" he asked.

"No," I responded.

"Their conventions are better than camp meetings," he added.

Better than camp meetings? I thought to myself. Hadn't he been to camp meetings and heard Elder H.M.S. Richards, Sr., and the King's Heralds from the Voice of Prophecy? Had he ever heard all those good speakers from the General Conference? Who can top camp meeting? But he had said, "It's better than camp meeting." His statement made me curious, and it stuck in my mind for many years. What could possibly happen at those conventions to make them better than camp meeting?

During my four years at Paradise Valley Hospital and four years pastoring the El Cajon church, I did not read or hear anything more about ASI. However, my curiosity about this lay organization was still lying dormant. I did not yet know even one person who was a member of ASI. Henry Martin, an ASI member, once said jokingly, "ASI is the best-kept secret in the Adventist Church."

2

" Oh, By the Way, Ken"

The next time I heard anything about ASI was when Elder John Osborn, the president of the Southeastern California Conference, met me in the hall of the conference office and said, "Oh, by the way, Ken, you are also the secretary of ASI."

This was six months after I had been elected secretary of Personal Ministries. When I found the ASI membership directory, it listed twenty-two members in our conference. I also found that since the directory had been printed, the membership had "grown" from twenty-two to eighteen.

I still knew very little about the organization. If you don't know very much about a subject, you had better begin to find out in a hurry. I thought that January would be a good time to let the members educate and train me about ASI and its purposes and objectives.

The first visit I made to an ASI member was to the Mobile X-ray Company, owned and operated by Earl and Fran Schoberth in Orange County. When I introduced myself as the new ASI secretary, Fran told me that Earl was busy taking x-rays at a school. Before I left, Fran, in her gentle way and with a smile, shared something with me.

"Elder Livesay, we have been giving Bibles studies to our neighbors. They have recently been baptized and become Adventists."

I cannot describe how this pleasant visit affected my soul! Business and professional people are very busy in their schedules, so I made visits appropriate to their business activities. During the next week, I visited all of the ASI members on the directory list. What a blessing and encouragement they were to me!

I discovered that our ASI members were very outreach oriented. I found that they were dedicated church members who were responsible leaders in their congregations. These families were Sabbath School teachers, elders, deacons or deaconesses, and missionary leaders. Many of them had introduced employees, neighbors, and friends to Jesus. My heart was thrilled by these visits! I knew that this organization held great potential for outreach.

During my visits over the next year I described to other professional and business families what I had found in my contacts with ASI members. Many of those I spoke with wanted to become members. Wonderful things began to happen! ASI membership grew steadily in our conference.

The following January, I visited the members again. Since I was now returning for a second year, they welcomed me with enthusiasm, warmth, and hospitality. Let me tell you, this work was fun! Business and professional people are a different segment of society. They must be on the cutting edge to survive the competition. During our visits I would share personal evangelism experiences of other ASI members. And as our visits closed, we prayed together.

Dr. William Shepherd, who did special visitation for the Pacific Union Conference, joined me the next January in visiting ASI members. He was a retired educator who had been president of three of our colleges and was the former ASI secretary for the Pacific Union. He enjoyed ASI, and he liked to call on members. So we had a great, enjoyable experience together!

Sensing the need to draw the ASI members together, we began an annual banquet that took place a few days before the Christmas holidays. These dinners were well attended, and the fellowship was great. Following the meal, we would interview some of our ASI members about their outreach experiences. Since outreach is the purpose of ASI, this feature was the icing on the cake. Nothing is as exciting to Seventh-day Adventists as knowing that the work of God is growing and doing well. Lay members are greatly stimulated by witnessing experiences. I have heard people say, "If this person can witness or study with someone, maybe I can too."

About 1965, I was junior camp pastor for a week at Pine Springs Ranch. On Saturday evenings, Elder Bill Dopp, the youth leader of the Southeastern California Conference, interviewed several young people around the campfire. He usually began the interview with the question, "Are you born again?" He chose those young people whom he knew were having a personal experience with Jesus.

I sat in the back row listening to these refreshing testimonies. I was so moved by these young people and their experiences that I discovered tears running down my face. It dawned on me that if I were moved like this, perhaps my church members would be affected as I had been. I began interviewing, once a month during the Sabbath morning worship service, new Christians who were having a wonderful experience with the Lord. The results brought a great blessing to my church. And it was the success of this monthly testimony time that led me to try something similar at our annual ASI banquet. As expected, it resulted in a wonderful spirit among our ASI members!

By 1976, ASI membership in our conference had grown to sixty-six. Dr. Shepherd and I called at the office of Tom and Vi Zapara. They had been members less than a year. Tom challenged me with a question: "Why don't we do something a little special in ASI?"

Later, as Elder Shepherd and I drove to our next visit, I asked him, "Why don't we get thirty-four new applications for membership by the time we go to the Pacific Union ASI chapter meeting in April?" We could then be the first conference to have 100 ASI members! We began contacting potential members. When we attended the convention in April, we surprised the union ASI secretary with enough new applications to make up 103 members. This came as a surprise to everyone, since no one knew we had met our objective. By 1981, ASI membership in the Southeastern California Conference had grown to 164—28 percent of the national membership total!

We encouraged our ASI members to attend the spring chapter meeting and also the national convention in the fall. None of the members seemed fully to understand what ASI was all about until they had attended an ASI convention. In our annual visits with ASI members, we encouraged them to become involved in outreach, using literature, personal witnessing, or other methods of their own choice. Dr. Shepherd and I heard expressed time and again the appreciation of members for what the conference was doing to show an interest in them. I came to see an ASI secretary as a chaplain to the members of this dynamic association of lay business people.

3

The Genesis of ASI

Tracing the beginnings of Adventist-Laymen's Services and Industries uncovers a fascinating background. A number of historical sources confirm that God was calling for mission service to be opened in the southern states. In 1883, when Pastor Corliss gave his report from that area, there were only 267 white and twenty black Sabbathkeepers in the entire south.

Louis A. Hansen, in his book *So Small a Dream*, states that there was no formal educational system in some of the rural and mountain areas of the southern states. A great need existed for instruction in healthful living, education, and spiritual values. *Origin and History of Seventh-day Adventists*, vol. 3, by Elder Arthur W. Spalding, provides an excellent background on the beginning of Madison College, as well as the founding of other self-supporting institutions. *Madison, God's Beautiful Farm*, by Ira Gish and Harry Christman, also describes the establishing of Madison College and explores its mission.

From the beginning the work of the lay members in the

> Seventh-day Adventist Church had counted as greatly as had the work of the preachers, in bringing the light of the gospel to the world and increasing the membership of the church. Stephen N. Haskell was convinced and won by a tract handed to him by William Saxby, a mechanic. The colporteur work and the medical and nursing work have evolved into professions in which considerable portions of the church members employ their full time. There remains the great mass of the people who earn their livelihood through secular occupations, but, with varying degrees of skill and devotion, give their time to the art of literature distribution, healing and benevolence . . .
>
> So many individuals, indeed, have given all to the work; the majority have given a little, and in times of emergency, more, but have still devoted nine tenths of their resources to the life of this earth. They needed, and they still need to understand what total spiritual warfare means; the devotion of all their resources; not tithe only, but the whole of their means; not just a Sabbath day's service, but the service of the entire week; not a graham loaf and a fomentation merely, but public demonstration and teaching of how to live; not the fourth commandment only, but an application of Christ's two great laws; not only the education of their own children, vital and deep though that be, but an educational influence going through the whole community and land; not a supporting clergy only, but a devotion of themselves, body, soul and spirit, to completion of the gospel work. Hence the message of the Spirit of Prophecy. Such a family or such a group, consecrated to the finishing of God's work, will make their family occupation the medium of salvation. Like (William) Carey, their business is to impart the gospel; they cobble shoes only to pay expenses.[1]

Also from the beginning, the Lord's messenger emphasized that the work is not to be "ours" and "yours" to distinguish service to be rendered by denominationally employed workers and self-supporting labors. It is all, under God, to be "our work." We're to be "workers together for God," as Paul describes it.

> The work is one. The objectives are one. The methods are the same. I find no special counsels delineating minutely how the self-supporting worker shall labor. There are no two lines of the Spirit of Prophecy counsel.[2]

Different lines of missionary work were to be engaged in by self-supporting workers, according to Ellen White. First and always, soul winning was and is to be made paramount. She emphasized the literature ministry.[3] Diet and healthful cooking were to be given their proper place in the sun.[4] The temperance message was to be proclaimed.[5] Health reform was to be recommended.[6] Health restaurants were to be opened.[7] Sanitariums were to be established.[8] Health food stores were to be operated.[9]

The philosophy of self-supporting work in the Seventh-day Adventist church is founded upon the concept that every member added to the ranks by conversion should be a worker for God. Ellen White wrote, "There is a place for everybody in the work. We each have a work to do whatever may be our occupation."[10] This was the philosophy and the mandate to found and operate a special school, which developed into Madison College.

> The beginnings of an organized effort to marshal the lay members of the church to all-out consecration of their time, strength, money, and devotion to the gospel work, and concerted group action to make this effort more telling, is seen in the movement begun in the southern United States and into overseas lands.[11]

Dr. E.A. Sutherland was the first president of Walla Walla College when the school opened its doors for academic studies in 1892. One of the first things he did was to instruct the faculty regarding the principles God had given this church through Mrs. White. After three years as president of Walla Walla College, he was asked to be the new president of Battle Creek College. Dr. Sutherland

and his old friend, Percy T. Magan, were working together again.

Their experience in the field of education had included work at Union College, Walla Walla College, and Battle Creek College. Both of these men had met rigid resistance in their efforts to reform Christian education as outlined by Sister White. In fact, it was these brethren who took the initiative to move Battle Creek College from Battle Creek to Berrien Springs, Michigan. Sutherland and Magan had experienced hardship and difficulty in establishing other schools. They were the men God was preparing for the purpose of a new venture in Christian education.

For about fifteen years, Dr. Sutherland had held deep convictions about the philosophy of Christian education, but he was unable to initiate them. He firmly believed that education was more than simply memorizing facts and figures. He believed that education taught people how to live. The faculty of the new Madison School would develop the work-study program Sutherland was convinced the Spirit of Prophecy outlined.

> In the spring of 1904 President E. A. Sutherland and Dean P.T. Magan, of Emmanuel Missionary College, were stirred by the appeals which for several years had been coming to the Seventh-day Adventist Church from Mrs. White, to make more decided efforts to assist in the needs of the South and to carry to it the last gospel message. There had been correspondence and personal conversations about the establishing of a special school. They proposed to cut loose from their responsibilities in the North and to enter upon the work in the South. As James Edson White had for a decade been leading in Seventh-day Adventist efforts for the evangelization and educational betterment of the colored people, they felt that they should apply themselves to the help and uplifting of the poorer classes of white people, and especially of the underprivileged strata of the mountain country. Mrs. White encouraged their resolution. There was, however, a decided but unspoken difference between

> their concept and hers. So far as the project had taken definite form in their minds, they thought of going up into the hill country, purchasing a small farm, perhaps in eastern Tennessee or North Carolina which their modest resources would permit, and there doing a purely local work for the community. She, viewing the large capacities and broad experience of the men, saw rather the need of establishing a training school for many workers who should go out to fill the needs of the whole land.[12]

It was the vision of Sutherland and Magan to establish a school where the science of true education might be taught. They traveled to Nashville, Tennessee, in June 1904 to board the riverboat *Morning Star* for a trip up the Cumberland River. Mrs. White was visiting her son James Edson, who was operating the riverboat as an outreach project in the south.

On this trip Edson White was looking for a suitable site on which to build an educational facility to train black workers. Sutherland and Magan were looking for a site to establish a training school for young white workers.

The first day there was a light breakdown in the boat's machinery, and they tied up for repairs at Edgefield Junction Landing, some twelve miles in a direct line from Nashville. W.O. Palmer, a helper of J.E. White, took Mrs. White up on the bank of the river, and pointed out to her an adjoining plantation which was for sale and which he and J.E. White had been considering. This was called the Nelson Place, after an early settler, but was now owned by a family named Ferguson. Palmer described the farm to her. It contained 414 acres and bordered the river, where the bottom was good soil, but the upland was poor and washed until its bare limestone rock cropped out nearly everywhere. But Mrs. White seemed impressed with the description.

> The next morning she called Sutherland and Magan to her room, and she said to them, "There is a farm here which the Lord wants you to have to start your school.

Well, they had heard of it, and they were not impressed. They did not like the description of the outcropping rock, nor the location, nor the size of the place, or the price, $12,700.[13]

The two men told Mrs. White that purchasing the property was out of the question. The farm was too large, and they didn't have any money to purchase the place. Besides this, they pointed out, the farm was a pile of rocks. But Sister White told them that this was the place the Lord wanted them to have. The record states that Sutherland and Magan "sat down on a rock and wept."[14] Through much negotiating, the farm was finally purchased for $12,723, which included all the stock and implements.

On October 1, 1904, the Adventists took possession of the 414-acre farm. Besides his wife, Sally, Sutherland brought M. Bessie DeGraw, Mrs. Nellie Druillard, Percy Magan, and Elmer Brink, whose skill in dairy management probably saved their lives. They established a school called the Nashville Agricultural and Normal Institute. By the spring of 1905, the student body had grown to fifteen. Students and faculty worked together to set out apple, peach, pear, and plum trees. The plan was to train the youth how to be self-supporting, how to do missionary outreach, and in practical life skills.

Everyone worked, even the president and the dean. They had to, for their very existence depended upon making the institution self-supporting from the beginning.

By 1910, school expenses were calculated at $10.50 a month. Teachers' salaries were $13 a month. Before academy and college work were added to the curriculum, the institution operated as a "special school." Here youth were trained to serve as "self-supporting missionary teachers and workers."[15]

The school grew and prospered. Students without money came from the four corners of the earth. With hard work, prayer, faith, and endurance, the faculty began to train and prepare young men and women to fill places in God's work. Many young people entered the medical work, self-supporting and missionary outreach, and denominational employment.

Of this new venture, Sister White wrote:

> I have been shown that in our educational work we are not to follow the methods that have been adopted in our older established schools. It was presented to me that this was a place where an all-round education could be given advantageously to students who came from the North and the South for instruction. The class of education given at the Madison School is such as will be accounted a treasury of great value by those who take up missionary work in foreign fields. If more students in other schools received a similar training, we as a people would be a spectacle to the world, to angels, and men.[16]

Dr. Frank Knittel, then president of Southern Missionary College, in an address to the Layman's Foundation Convention of self-supporting workers in October 1973, declared:

> You have sought to enhance intellectual attainment in every way that you possibly could without sacrificing the moral and spiritual commitment which has prompted your work . . . There was a time when Madison College had the finest roster of teachers found anywhere within the denominational educational system. There was a core of teachers at Madison College which, with their training and experience, represented a greater assembly of advanced degrees than the rest of Seventh-day Adventist colleges put together.[17]

In 1930, Madison School became Madison College. Between the years 1930 and 1950, Madison enjoyed a "golden age." The press gave lasting and favorable publicity. In the May 1938 issue of *Reader's Digest*, Weldon Melisk explained in most laudatory terms the principles on which the school operated. Applications to attend Madison College poured in from India, Africa, Turkey, China, Russia—from everywhere.

In June 1938 the *New York Times* sent a photographer and a reporter to the campus to capture the spirit of the school. On October 7, 1938, Eleanor Roosevelt wrote of Madison College in glowing terms in her column, "My Day." Governor Frank G. Clement of Tennessee said, "It is refreshing to find a college operating on a self-supporting basis. The state of Tennessee needs more schools like Madison College."

By 1910 there were fifty small schools or health units in seven southern states operating as self-supporting mission stations. The first convention of self-supporting institutions met at Madison College in 1908 to encourage one another and to lay plans for making a wider impact. Our present ASI national conventions trace their origins to these early conventions.

The story of Madison College and its pioneers would fill volumes in detailing the providences of God. Only eternity will reveal the impact of Madison's influence on the South and on the world. During my years at the General Conference in the ASI office, everywhere I traveled I met former students still talking about their experience at Madison College. The education they received at Madison prepared them well for leadership in the service of the church.

> Once a year for forty years, the schools, sanitariums, rest homes, and other enterprises of the rural missions have joined in a self-supporting worker's convention, held at Madison College. This is under the auspices of the Laymen's Extension League, a loose confederation of units, with a central core of organization which collates and dispenses information both in correspondence and in print, and which arranges the program of the convention.[18]

In the year 1946 the Southern Union Conference, under the impulsion of its president, E.F. Hackman, in conjunction with Madison College, initiated a movement to align the self-supporting units and the conference

> organization for more complete cooperation and extension of their work beyond the current borders. The General Conference was interested, and with the strong support of its president, J.L. McElhany, and the vice-president for North America, N.C. Wilson, there emerged a plan for united effort which envisages the enrollment of many more laymen—ideally in time, the whole membership—in such group missionary activities as have been demonstrated for forty years by the Southern self-supporting units.[19]

On March 4 and 5, 1947, in Cincinnati, Ohio, a group met for the purpose of organizing the Adventist self-supporting institutions. Following are three paragraphs from the minutes of that historic meeting:

> Through the courtesy of the Columbia Union Conference in session in the Gibson Hotel, Cincinnati, Ohio, representatives of some 25 self-supporting institutions met in the Roof Garden of the same hotel at ten o'clock on the morning of March 4, 1947, for the purpose of organizing the proposed Association of Seventh-day Adventist Self-Supporting Institutions.
>
> Dating back some two years, the General Conference of Seventh-day Adventists in Fall Council 1945, had recommended the organization of such an association as a means of uniting the self-supporting workers, encouraging the enlarging of this type of work and making possible a stronger tie between the self-supporting work and the regular organized work of the denomination.
>
> For the unifying and operating of the self-supporting units another organization was effected. The Seventh-day Adventist Association of Self-Supporting Institutions is a body composed of representatives from the General and Union conferences and the self-supporting units. Dr. E.A. Sutherland was the first president of ASI and Dr. Wayne McFarland the first secretary.[20]

Through the years, the vision that began at Madison has continued to grow in the cooperative efforts of the laymen and the church. The spirit of Madison continues to live. ASI has extended membership to Adventists who are in business and the professions to assist them in sharing the good news of the gospel of Jesus Christ. Men and women are talking with those who come to their garages, offices, farms and other places where they meet the public. ASI is growing rapidly, expanding now into countries other than the United States and Canada. The national and union chapters hold annual conventions. The purpose of ASI and its conventions is to plan and encourage missionary outreach. God is leading, and we are willing to follow.

The great gospel commission requires men, women, and youth to share the good news about Jesus Christ. The gospel calls for professionals, business persons, teachers, ministers, and everyone to stand together as one body of believers in telling of Christ's love for fallen people and of His willingness to forgive and accept sinners.

Looking ahead, we must ever remember these words of Ellen White: "We have nothing to fear for the future, except as we shall forget the way the Lord has led us, and His teaching in our past history."[21]

The officers and the members of ASI must remember that the organization was begun to spread the good news! God will continue to bless if we remember our mission!

Notes:

1. Arthur W. Spalding, *Origin and History of Seventh-day Adventists*, vol. 3, pp. 168, 169.
2. Arthur White, in a 1966 address to an ASI convention in Loma Linda, California.
3. *Testimonies for the Church*, vol. 4, p. 389.
4. *Testimonies for the Church*, vol. 7, p. 112.
5. Ibid., p. 115.
6. Ibid., p. 119.
7. Ibid., pp. 122, 123.
8. *Medical Ministry*, p. 306.
9. *Counsels to Parents, Teachers, and Students*, p. 495.

10. Ellen G. White, *Words for Encouraging Self-supporting Workers*, p. 11, as quoted by Robert H. Pierson in *Miracles Happen Every Day*, pp. 83, 84.
11. Spalding, op. cit.
12. Spalding, pp. 168-170.
13. Ibid., p. 171.
14. Ibid., p. 173.
15. Pierson, pp. 38, 39.
16. From a pamphlet published by Madison College and Sanitarium.
17. *Madison Survey*, December, 1973.
18. Spalding, p. 183.
19. Ibid., pp. 182, 183.
20. Ibid., pp. 184, 185.
21. *Life Sketches*, p. 196.

4

The Secret Is in the Convention

To attend an ASI national convention is almost like being at a family reunion. Warmth and camaraderie are much in evidence in the lobby of the convention site as members come together. Yes, there are happy greetings, hugs, and "holy kisses." Many of the members have been attending these conventions for several years. The ASI spirit is in full bloom for the entire four days.

Attendance at the conventions has grown so large that it is a problem finding sites to accommodate all those who wish to come. During the years I helped plan the conventions, we held one of them on the campus of Pacific Union College and another on the campus of Andrews University so that our members could see these fine schools. Another reason for meeting on these campuses was that the cost of lodging and food was well within the budget of everyone.

Careful plans must be made for a convention to set the

right tone for the meetings. Good music, excellent food, and ample time for fellowship are important for the four days. Since everyone enjoys good food, we always asked Paul Damazo, a professional dietitian, to work with chefs in the food planning. Many of the chefs needed help in preparing vegetarian menus. With Paul's expertise, we have enjoyed some great food!

ASI is always at its best when the theme of evangelism is the focus of the convocation. We always surveyed those who were in attendance at the convention to find out what they enjoyed most and what they felt was most helpful in the program. The survey results revealed that the programs on witnessing scored higher than all other events.

For as long as I can remember, ASI members have wanted to support some special mission project. This idea arose spontaneously from the laymen, not from the organized church. Traditionally, an offering was taken or pledges were made to support a specific project. In many cases these offerings were for some self-supporting ministry that needed a boost. Initially, these offerings totaled about $20,000.

Following the national convention in 1980, two ASI members, Tom Zapara and Harold Lance, got into a private discussion about these offerings. Their conclusion was that $20,000 wasn't very much, considering the resources of the members. After some planning during the following year, they decided that these support offerings could easily reach $100,000. At the next convention, the offering amounted to well over $100,000. In recent years, these support efforts have been ranging from $250,000 to $450,000.

Adventist people will be generous when there is a known need. I remember at one of the conventions when a business man stated that God had blessed his business with profits of several million dollars, and he wanted to wisely distribute this to support the cause of God. That is the spirit of ASI.

The Pacific Union was the first to form an ASI chapter. Elder Miller Brockett, the ASI secretary, planned a meeting for ASI members to meet at Wawona Youth Camp in 1973. This convention was for the purpose of studying the possibility of forming a chapter. ASI members from the North Pacific Union were also invited. Attendance was good and the spirit of the meeting was excellent. Officers were chosen, and the first union chapter was formed. By 1983 every union had formed a chapter. Sometime later, the Canadian Union formed its chapter, and recently it has divided into two chapters.

It is my opinion that establishing the union chapters has been a giant step forward for ASI. Almost everyone can attend a spring chapter meeting. This has exposed more and more qualified people to the outreach objectives and purposes of ASI. Membership has grown, and more people are attending the national conventions.

The spirit of an ASI convention is difficult to adequately describe. Reading written accounts of these meetings is not enough to communicate what is really happening in these convocations. For example, at the 1992 convention, Bob Slikkers, owner of the S2 Yacht Company, told how he was inspired to begin a Daniel Seminar after hearing others tell of their experience at an ASI convention. The only way anyone can understand and experience the spirit of ASI is to personally attend a convention!

I have always believed that God called me to the ministry to be effective in preparing people for eternal life. I discovered that much of this dream was fulfilled by serving as an ASI secretary. It opened many areas for helping others to be missionaries in their own sphere of influence. My conference president once asked me, "How much time are you spending with ASI?" My answer was that only about 5 percent of my time was required. For, you see, as a rule business and professional people are leaders. It takes little time or effort to pass along a vision to laymen who are leaders.

While serving in the national office in Washington D.C., I received a letter one day from a member who asked why he should continue his membership. The answer was simple. I wrote to him about what happens in my own soul as I experience the vitalizing Spirit of God speaking to me at the conventions. It has always been this way!

Elder Robert S. Folkenberg was one of the speakers at the 1992 convention in Palm Springs, California. On August 11, 1992, he wrote this memo to the conference presidents:

> The largest convention ever held in ASI's 45-year history convened at Palm Springs, California, August 5-8. ASI's motto, "Sharing Christ in the Marketplace," came alive in the personal and soul-winning testimonies shared by many laymen. It is an exhilarating experience to spend time with our loyal dedicated laity whose demonstrated primary objective is sharing their joy in Christ with others. How I pray that every member could catch the same vision.

Elder Alfred McClure, President of the North American Division, commented, "I wish every SDA in North America could be a member of ASI."

Visitors came from as far away as Africa, India, and Europe. And you, too, are invited to attend a convention and catch the ASI spirit!

5

Hammers-and-Saws Evangelism

Following his discharge from military service after World War II, John Freeman and his wife, Ida Mae, moved to Berrien Springs, Michigan. Over the ensuing years, we became friends. John and Ida Mae have always been adventurous and innovative. They were a young couple who loved the Lord, the church, and people. The Freemans went into the publishing business. John's business took him all over North America, as well as to other interesting places. The Freemans had a dream about lay witnessing that has become a fascinating story.

In early 1969 a Caribbean cruise line enlisted John's services to produce a brochure advertising the convention potential of Jamaica's picturesque harbors—including scenes someone would have to photograph from the air.

He flew from Miami to Jamaica on a Friday. Wishing to be with those of his own faith on Sabbath, he phoned the Andrews Memorial Hospital to arrange a room for the weekend. The hospital was full, but the medical director invited him to stay in his home. His weekend with Dr. Fowler, the director, would later result in the birth of Maranatha Flights International.

"We are trying to work out an interesting project that will be a great blessing to the patients in our hospital," Fowler began.

"Yes?" John replied, only mildly interested.

"You see, a student and a faculty member from Southern Missionary College have volunteered to come to Jamaica this summer and install a public address system in our hospital. With this facility we can provide good music for our patients, and they will also be able to hear the Sabbath morning services as well as the talks our chaplain gives each day. We believe it can be a real missionary venture."

"How is the project coming?" Freeman asked.

"I have made all the necessary arrangements with the government, and I have all work permits in hand. But we have one immediate problem," Dr. Fowler explained. "We don't have the money for the fares of the two men from Southern Missionary College or funds to bring the equipment to Kingston."

Thinking It Over in Flight

A few days later, as John Freeman relaxed on an Air Jamaica jet enroute back to Miami, Dr. Fowler's words kept running through his mind. Sick patients. Missionary opportunities. Equipment. Available personnel. Fares. Funds.

John wanted to accept the challenge of providing help in transporting the two Southern Missionary College men to Andrews Memorial Hospital in Jamaica. He decided to approach the owner of the cruise ship to see if he would help.

During their conversation, the owner told John that his principal business was making cookies. John asked him if he knew the McKee family, who were also in the cookie business. The gentleman replied that he knew not only the McKees, but two other Adventist businessmen who were in the cookie business.

The cruise ship owner thought so highly of the integrity of these three Adventist businessmen that he gladly donated two tickets for passage on his ship so the two men from SMC could volunteer their time for a much-needed electronics project at the hospital in Jamaica.

"There must be projects in other needy places like this one in Kingston," John mused, "and there must be committed laymen in the Seventh-day Adventist church and other Christian churches—like the two men from Southern Missionary College—who would respond to similar challenges and give their time and expertise providing help in mission lands. Some lay organization should be on the job arranging the details. The denomination, through its regular channels, is doing a great job meeting the endless needs in many parts of the world," he thought. "But there must be some way we laymen can pitch in and help them more."

"It must be a laymen's program," he told himself as his plane flew high over Cuba and the Gulf of Mexico. "Volunteers would serve for a couple of weeks or so during their vacations, or even after their retirement—any time at their convenience."

The idea rapidly took shape as he pondered the potential of such a program. Such volunteers would pay their own expenses to the place of service. The mission field, benefiting from their help, should be willing to pick up the tab for room and board in return for a good day's work. Teams could fly to mission stations and do all sorts of needed jobs. They could help erect and remodel buildings or care for neglected maintenance chores. Women could help, too, by teaching sewing and cooking classes. They could buy the food and cook it. And they could even help with construction.

Many of the volunteers, he decided, would be young people. "Youth welcome a challenge," he reassured himself as his plane came in for a landing at the Miami airport. "They won't mind roughing it a bit."

Then, too, young and old would be able to experience the thrill of visiting new lands, meeting new people, and seeing new sights. After forty hours of work a week, they would be entitled to a bit of sightseeing, and of socializing and fraternizing with the local people. Freeman was certain there would be Seventh-day Adventists and other Christians who would be thrilled at the prospect of such an adventure and an opportunity to serve.

Some hours later, when John arrived back home in Berrien Springs, Michigan, he had the basics of a new laymen's service plan fairly well in his mind. Eager to see his new dream become a reality, John talked the program over with his wife, Ida Mae, and his secretary, Margie Tessner. Both agreed it was a great idea to work on.

With John Freeman, decision meant action. He secured a copy of the latest denominational yearbook, where he found the names and addresses of union and mission leaders in the Inter-American Division. He decided to write letters to them, explaining the program he had in mind for willing laymen.

Was his plan practical? he asked them. Would it be helpful?

The response was excellent. The prospect of receiving more help for their almost endless needs thrilled the men. Their mission budgets were never able to accomplish all that they needed to do. Anything a new laymen's organization could do to supplement the regular church-supported projects would be greatly appreciated. When could the first volunteers arrive?

"Send them as quickly as you can!" the mission leaders responded. "We need churches, schools, youth camps, welfare centers, first-aid stations, hospitals, and outpatient clinics. Send your builders, your plumbers and painters, your electricians, your bulldozer operators. We can use linguists, teachers, Bible instructors, typists, and many more. Send them all—and quickly!"

John Freeman got the message. The needs were many. Now, who would fill them?

He wrote to many of his friends, asking if they would be willing to spend two or three weeks of their annual vacations helping in various overseas projects. Those with planes would fly them at their own expense, taking volunteers to prearranged building projects.

John's friends quickly responded to the challenge. Immediately, John, Ida Mae, and Margie Tessner commenced to draw up plans for a nonprofit corporation.

Getting Things Organized

What would be an appropriate and challenging name for the new organization? "Most people are intrigued with flying," John thought, "especially if it leads to adventure in exotic lands. Young people, too, must be challenged to participate. And the name must include a spiritual emphasis."

"*Maranatha* means 'Lord, come!' in Aramaic." Margie Tessner suggested. "The main objective of the new organization will be to tell people this blessed truth. Why not include Maranatha in the name?"

The Freemans agreed.

"We want to include the idea of flying to foreign countries—even faraway lands someday," John added. "This will challenge the older and the young alike. Why not call our program Maranatha Flights International?" he asked. "We can make it a Christian peace corps."

They soon realized, as they sought counsel, that to be a non-profit organization, they needed to obtain this status with the Internal Revenue Service.

Thus Marshall Meyers from Washington, D. C. came into the Maranatha picture at a crucial time in its history. John flew to Washington and explained the whole Maranatha concept to Meyers.

"I can do it for you," the attorney told him. "It will cost you $1,600 to receive your tax-exempt status." Then followed a cordial discussion as John enlarged on his hopes and plans for Maranatha Flights International.

Within about ninety days, Maranatha had IRS approval. Several years after Attorney Meyers had worked out the Maranatha problems with the IRS, John wrote to me. "I wish we could thank Marshall Meyers enough for all that he has done to help us. To date he has never sent us a bill for his invaluable services."

During the early days of Maranatha's history, the organization operated out of the Freeman's home. John's secretary cared for all of the MFI correspondence and other work. And Freeman paid most of the expense out of his own pocket.

John and Ida Mae made great sacrifices to fulfill their dream for this outreach. Each year MFI required more and more of John's time. He had an Aztec plane that he used for his personal work. Finally, because of the mounting expenses of MFI, the Freemans decided to sell their plane. First, John made adjustments in his twenty-employee shop. Then he closed it, sold the building, and jobbed out his printing. Sometimes dreams are expensive, but the mission is worth it!

During the Christmas holidays in 1969, John and Ida Mae had flown friends to Freeport on Grand Bahama Island for a brief vacation. The group rented motorcycles and set out to see the sights. One day as they cycled the roads of Grand Bahama, they passed a half-built church by the roadside.

The building was abandoned. Weeds flourished both inside and outside the unfinished walls. It had no roof and no doors—only gaping holes where windows should have been. A sign, half hidden in the weeds, announced to all who passed by that this unfinished place of worship belonged to local Seventh-day Adventists. The partially completed shell distressed the visitors from America.

Returning to Freeport, the Freemans and their party attended the local church on Sabbath. "What happened out at Eight Mile Rock?" they asked the young pastor, Anthony Modell.

"Oh, the pastor moved away," Modell replied, "and the people became discouraged. The unfinished church has been sitting there for more than a year now."

"What are your plans for the future?" Freeman pressed.

"Well, I guess we don't have any plans right now. The people have lost interest. We don't know what the mission committee plans to do next. Maybe just let it stand."

Maranatha Members Move In

The little band of Adventist visitors held a committee meeting of their own and reached a unanimous decision. Completion of the Eight Mile Rock church would be their first project. They would undertake it during the upcoming Christmas vacation.

Soon they talked with Pastor Modell again.

"How would you like for a group of us to come down during the upcoming Christmas holidays and help you finish your Eight Mile Rock church?" they asked.

Plans were made with the local congregation, and the first MFI project was on.

Back home once more, John's secretary sent out letters bubbling with enthusiasm. Twenty-eight people responded for this first project. The work party included a number of young people from Andrews University. The local church cooperated, their hearts filled with joy. The Maranatha team completed the Eight Mile Rock Church during the allotted Christmas holiday, to the joy of the 210 members. So the first project went as planned, and God's work was given a great boost! With this beginning, Maranatha was off and running with a dream—in the true spirit of ASI!

Recently, Elder Robert S. Folkenberg, president of the General Conference of Seventh-day Adventists, paid tribute to the 22,512 volunteers of MFI who have traveled to

186 countries worldwide to help in constructing buildings for the church. During the years of MFI's outreach, 6,000 youth have participated in almost 500 projects. There have been 1,369,241 hours of donated labor to construct churches on almost every continent and on many islands of the sea. MFI has rebuilt homes destroyed by earthquakes in several locations. Hospitals have also been the focus of their efforts in many parts of the world.

In the book *Here Comes Adventure*, by Robert H. Pierson, a page dedicated to the Freeman family reads as follows:

> To John D. Freeman—Mr. Maranatha—founder and president of Maranatha Flights International, for his tireless commitment to the development of this Christian peace corps, and to Ida Mae Freeman—Mrs. Maranatha—copilot and loyal supporter of this international missionary endeavor, and to the five Freeman daughters—Kathy Clough, Melody Durham, April Stevenson, Cherry Brooks, and Jonna Davis—for their understanding and cooperation during years when it sometimes meant sharing Dad with needy areas far from home, and to "John's Bunch"—those stalwart Maranatha leaders who have given so unstintingly of their time, their talent, and their treasure to make Maranatha Flights International the potent factor for good in the world that it has become, *Here Comes Adventure* is appreciatively dedicated.

Since 1983, Don Noble has served as president of MFI. Under his skilled leadership, the work has continued to expand. In 1989, Maranatha moved its headquarters to Sacramento, California, and changed its name to Maranatha Volunteers International. At this writing, Maranatha has completed over 700 projects valued at over $27 million. The membership at the present time is over 8,000, representing all 50 states and 44 foreign countries. New dreams and plans that have been carried out are almost beyond human imagination!

Santo Domingo '92

When Adventist journals began to publish information about the Santo Domingo project—"25 churches in 70 days"—it fired the imagination of the Adventist church! Coordinating the individual church sites, appealing to the 1,200 people who came to work, getting the building materials, and getting the shipping containers released at the last minute was more than human effort! God was certainly leading Maranatha Volunteers!

Maranatha Volunteers International became a member of ASI in 1973. MVI has distinguished itself and has been an honor to ASI. Thirty-five ASI dads and their sons traveled to the project at their own expense in February of 1992 to help build two churches in Savica and Palma I. These kinds of programs make a difference with dads and sons—and the world! Maranatha's membership has added much to the spirit of ASI!

6

Examples of the ASI Spirit

Who are these interesting people who have such a love for God and the church? What is it that causes them to have such a loyalty to the great gospel commission? Let's look at the diversity of their occupations, businesses, and professions. Perhaps their expertise in leadership also causes them to be successful in their dedication to God.

ASI members own and/or operate nursing homes, medical and dental offices and labs, chiropractic offices, health reconditioning centers, and hospitals. They practice law and have counseling offices. They manufacture and market candles, health food, baked goods, cabinets, and picture frames. They are in plumbing, electrical, logging, and building companies. They operate restaurants, travel agencies, carpet and interior decorating stores, and insurance agencies. They produce radio and television programs and own broadcasting stations. They are ranchers, dairymen, and honey farmers. They have automobile dealerships, automotive repair and body shops, tire stores, and photography studios. And the list is only beginning.

Let's consider the outreach activities of some members of ASI.

How would you like to visit a lawyer for legal advice and end up having him pray with you? This happens in many Adventist attorney's offices. I became acquainted with such a lawyer, Harold Lance, in 1966. A spiritual renewal was taking place in the Lance family. As we visited in my office, I began to talk to Harold about ASI. I thought that he and his wife, Joan, would appreciate the spiritual tone of the organization.

In 1976, they attended a Pacific Union Conference ASI chapter meeting. Life for Harold and Joan has not been the same since that weekend. They returned home, and their pastor asked Harold to tell the church about the ASI convention. This talk influenced eleven families in the Ontario, California, Adventist church to join ASI.

Harold was elected president of ASI for the North American Division at the national convention in 1979. During his next four years as president, he traveled the United States, making new friends with many Adventists. During his tenure of office, ASI was invited to come to the British Union to organize the first overseas chapter.

Later, Harold was asked to serve on the executive board of Outpost Centers, Inc. OCI is a world-wide lay support ministry with a home office in Dunlap, Tennessee. When it became known in 1988 that Warren Wilson, the president of OCI, was terminally ill, the board asked Harold to be the new president of OCI. Harold followed the example of the apostle Paul. He left his practice of law to become a full-time worker in lay ministry. When Harold and I talked about this new position, he said, "This is the first time I have been asked to work full time for the church." That is the spirit of ASI.

Showroom Witnessing

In 1976, Elder Phil Dunham invited me to assist him for a weekend of lay training at the Gladstone campground in Oregon. This was a delightful experience—meeting more Adventists. After the Saturday evening training session, Henry Martin introduced himself, and the next morning I met his wife, Robin.

Auto Martin, Limited, was one of the oldest Mercedes-Benz dealerships in the United States and had been an ASI member since 1970. And I had met Henry's father at a national ASI convention in San Diego in 1971. So the Martin family of Grants Pass, Oregon, was not new to me. We spent some time visiting about his business and about ASI.

Ruth and I have ever since enjoyed a long and lasting friendship with Henry and Robin.

After their conversion in 1975, Henry and Robin became greatly interested in witnessing for Christ. Adventist literature was as visible in their showroom as were Volvos, Nissans, and Mercedes-Benzs. Henry, Robin, and their children are available to share Jesus anywhere, anytime. The family has actively served on nine Maranatha projects.

Several who have worked for the Martins have become Adventist Christians because of their witness. In one year alone, eight of their employees and customers became Adventists. One night, the janitor's wife picked up a piece of literature from Henry's office desk and read it. When she went home that night, she studied the literature and her Bible for hours. She visited the Adventist church the next Sabbath morning. When Henry greeted her at the front door of the church, she told him what had happened in his office and why she was in church. As time went by, she received Bible studies, and she and her two daughters were baptized.

"It is interesting," Henry noted, "that she would have a master key to enter in the middle of the night and discover a Bible study tract to study by herself. She admitted enjoying various pieces of literature from the waiting room rack in previous months."

One day a former Adventist phoned Henry about purchasing a Mercedes-Benz. As Henry talked to this potential customer about his motives for buying such a car, he appealed to him to come back to the Lord, for Jesus was coming soon. The gentleman changed his mind about purchasing a new Mercedes, but he did go back to church.

When the North Pacific Union chapter was organized, Henry was chosen to be the first president. He also served on the national executive committee, then became national vice-president of ASI, and later was elected president.

Henry and Robin were daily seeking God's will for the future and were convicted they should enter Christian ministry on a full time volunteer basis. After much prayer and study, they sold Auto Martin in 1988. They moved to France to help in the Country Life Paris Restaurant. Since returning home, they have been serving at Weimar Institute, doing volunteer work and still sharing the Good News wherever they are! This, too, is the spirit of ASI!

Dorcas Is Still Busy!

Many who read this book may remember Aunt Sue of the "Your Story Hour" children's radio program. ASI remembers her for the community service work she and her husband, Ralph, carried out in Medina, Ohio. When Betty's parents, Mr. and Mrs. Ray Ahnsted, moved to Medina, there wasn't an Adventist church in town. They began to conduct Sabbath School and worship services in their home. As the new church grew, they eventually built a sanctuary.

Betty and her mother started the work of Community Services in their city. This ministry grew to the extent that it had to be moved to a larger building in the business section of Medina. The people of that city were so impressed with their ministry that Betty was invited to speak in churches, service clubs, and to other groups. When Ruth and I visited the Ahnbergs in 1980, Betty said that all of the churches in the city except two were helping the Community Service Center financially each month from their church budgets.

The president of one of the banks phoned Betty one day and asked her to stop by his office.

"We have been watching your work in this community for years," he told her. "There is a trust fund that was left in our bank to benefit needy people in Medina County. We want to help you with your work—what are your needs?" It took a minute for Betty to gather her wits. "This trust fund is substantial," he continued, "so don't think small." She told the banker that they needed a building in which to store furniture given to them and a van to move the furnishings. The banker told Betty to go to the Chevrolet agency and order the van that would be adequate for her work. He would instruct the agency to send the bill to the bank. A building was also acquired for their storage purposes. The banker added, "We don't need any receipts, because we trust Adventists."

During our visit to Medina, Betty took me to visit several people to whom they had given assistance. They had become Adventist Christians because of the love and dignity they had experienced at the Community Service Center. I must add that several of the volunteers from other churches who helped at the Center also became Adventists.

One experience she shared with us, I will never forget. A Jewish lady had come to the Center to talk about a financial problem in her family. She had assets, but because of a temporary problem, was unable to pay her utility bills, and termination of her service was threatened. Betty treated this lady with Christian dignity in this traumatic situation. She assured her that the Center would help her by paying the utility bills.

Before the woman left Betty's office, Betty prayed with

her. At the end of the prayer, the lady was weeping because of the kindness and love shown to her. Betty threw her arms around her to comfort her as she cried. Two weeks later, this lady returned with one request: "Betty, would you hug me again?" Many of you know that Betty and Ralph have fallen asleep in Jesus. The Ahnbergs embodied the spirit of ASI!

Ten years ago, a number of theology students graduating from Andrews University had not been hired for full-time ministry. Elder Charles Bradford, then vice-president of the North American Division, talked to me about an idea I thought was very good. He suggested that perhaps some of the ASI businessmen could hire some of these young men to work in their businesses and serve as chaplains to their employees.

In addition, they could give Bible studies and preach in some of the local churches on Sabbath. This would give the ministerial students additional practical experience that might increase their chances for denominational employment. Their services would be truly valuable to privately owned hospitals, nursing homes, or even some of the larger manufacturing companies.

I thought it was a great concept then, and I think it is still an excellent plan. The right person with theological training could be an asset both to the company and to the local church.

In the spring of 1983 as we began to attend the union chapter meetings, I threw out these possibilities. I covered some of the ideas just mentioned.

An ASI member in El Cajon, California, Dale McBride, was challenged by the possibilities of implementing this idea. This didn't surprise me, because Dale is a man who always sees positive opportunities—a man absolutely dedicated to God and to the church. I know, for I was his pastor for four years.

Dale went to Andrews University and placed a notice on the theological seminary bulletin board. He offered employment to ministerial students who would be willing to give Bible studies, help with vacation Bible schools, preach in local churches, and witness to his clients.

When he returned home, the phone began to ring. Several students wanted to work for him in his business and be involved in some form of outreach. Five young men benefited from this arrangement.

Recently I called Dale to find out what the results had been. He told me that two of these students are now working for the church as pastors. One of the others is privately employed and deeply committed to his local church, preaching on Sabbaths, giving Bible studies, and working in one of the health van programs. This is only one of the many things Dale and his wife, Barbara, are doing for their church and for the Lord. Another family demonstrating the ASI spirit!

7

ASI: Leading in Innovative Ideas

Inflation and interest rates were running as high as 22 percent in the 1970s. This posed a serious problem for those congregations planning to build a new church. The value of funds accumulating for a new church building was being rapidly eroded by runaway inflation. Conference policy requires that a congregation have 25 percent cash in hand before loans are made and before construction can begin. This is a sound and proven policy. But the problem was, how could new churches reach their financial goals and qualify for loans when dogged by high inflation?

About this time, my son, Don—a minister in the Georgia-Cumberland Conference—told me about a group of laymen there who had formulated a plan to help build new churches in their conference. They generated funds from gifts and donations from laymen. This group worked in harmony with the conference administration. When a congregation needed a new church and could meet the regular payments, it would receive a loan with low interest rates to build a new sanctuary. This plan had proven itself in the Georgia-Cumberland Conference for several years. Why wouldn't this idea work in the Southeastern California Conference?

I shared the plan with two ASI members in Southeastern who had open ears and thought it was a progressive idea. When the plan was presented to Elder Walter Blehm, the conference president, he thought we should adopt it for our people in the Southeastern California Conference.

The conference held a holiday ASI banquet in December each year. After everyone had eaten a delightful Chinese dinner, we shared the plan to help newly organized churches finance their sanctuaries. It was so well accepted that the presentation was finished in about ten minutes. Tom Zapara presented a motion that I should choose a committee to select a board of directors. The directors would form a new non-profit corporation. We chose those ASI members who had expertise in the fields of work that were needed. They were to form and operate the new corporation.

The directors chosen for the new venture included Leroy Luyster, CPA; Harold Lance, an attorney; Howard Voyles, a man in advertising; Maurice Giberson, a realtor; Sarah Deacon; Paul Damazo; Tom Zapara; Dr. Charles Brinegar; and myself as executive secretary.

The name chosen for the new corporation was S.D.A. Layman's New Church Development, Inc. Harold Lance led in forming the corporation, and Leroy Luyster contacted the Internal Revenue Service for the needed non-profit status. Our application to the IRS for nonprofit status was approved in May 1976.

The conference administration was pleased. Elder Walter Blehm wrote a letter to each Adventist family in the Southeastern California Conference describing the new corporation and its purposes and objectives. The conference agreed to assist new congregations by purchasing the property on which the new church would be built. They also sponsored banquets periodically and invited families to listen to the plan of financing the new churches.

When the laymen heard about the plan, they embraced the idea wholeheartedly. Donations began to come in for this exciting venture. The work of God was expanding!

A fast-growing Spanish church in San Ysidro, a city south of San Diego, was the first church to be the recipient of a low-interest loan to build a new sanctuary. The interest rate was 6 percent—very low for the 70s.

This plan has worked well in the Southeastern California Conference since 1976. We are grateful for the idea that originated in the Georgia-Cumberland Conference and that has made such a tremendous contribution to the work in Southeastern.

New Church Development, Inc., is still helping new churches and schools that need a boost to get started. Besides operating their own businesses and sharing the gospel, ASI members have helped launch a plan that has proven a great blessing to the work of God. More of the spirit of ASI in action!

Have Hammer and Saw, Will Build

John Freeman, introduced in Chaper 5, and who gave leadership in forming Maranatha Flights International, has been a friend of mine since 1947. His enthusiasm was something else as he told me on several occasions about building churches and schools with volunteers.

After funds were made available in Southeastern to help build new churches, I thought, "Why not take the next step? Form a Maranatha chapter in the conference and build these churches with volunteers!"

I phoned John and talked to him about the chapter idea. Naturally, he was enthusiastic.

I then phoned several building contractors, electricians, plumbers, and others in the building trades and shared what I had in mind. We called a meeting. Twenty-five builders came to the meeting on a Sunday evening to discuss the formation of a chapter of MFI that would build only in the Southeastern California Conference to help new congregations that needed a sanctuary.

Naturally, I explained, the builders would also be free to go on other MFI projects. But the group of builders chose rather to form their own organization of volunteers to build churches and schools only in our conference.

The new group of volunteer builders chose the name Maranatha Southeastern California; however, they voted not to become a chapter of Maranatha Flights International. Officers were chosen that evening.

Soon an article about the new organization appeared in the Pacific Union *Recorder*. Dental students of the class of 1980 from the Loma Linda University School of Dentistry had recently voted to give two weeks of their time to a mission project during their 1979 summer break. When they read in the *Recorder* about this new builders' group, they offered their services.

The Vista Adventist Samoan congregation was planning to build a sanctuary, and everything was ready for the first project. Vista was a convenient site for the dental students, being only sixty miles from Loma Linda.

Phase I of the building project was scheduled to begin on June 15 with the pouring of the foundation and the laying of block. Phase II would begin August 13, when the dental students would come to finish the church. Remarkably, thirty-five of the forty-five students had previous building experience! This was a tremendous help, and they enjoyed using their skills. The dental students donating their time to build the new church were a wonderful group of young men.

On Sabbath, August 25, Sabbath School and worship services were conducted in the new sanctuary. The new church seated 280 persons. It included an office, Sabbath School classrooms, and a baptistry, making a very nice complex for the congregation.

Sometime later, Paul Damazo approached me about the possibility of Maranatha Southeastern California expanding to be a union-wide organization. He said that there were at least fifty-seven churches in the Pacific Union that did not have a sanctuary for worship. We agreed that he had a good idea. So our Southeastern group of volunteers agreed to set up a Pacific Union Conference organization for a wider field of service.

Some of us met to organize a volunteer group to build churches and schools in the Pacific Union. What would be an appropriate name for the volunteer builders? We wanted a name that encompassed the concept of supporting new mission churches. So it was that another new organization was born, called ASI Mission Church Builders. We knew we would have the support of the union ASI chapter. And the Pacific Union Conference administration also gave full support to the new organization.

Plans moved quickly, and MCB built its first church in February 1980 in Boulder, Nevada. After over twelve years of building in the Pacific Union, ASI Mission Church Builders has completed 53 projects, using 3,995 volunteers, for a total of 412,687 square feet. It has donated 1,037,290 hours of labor worth an estimated $27,966,290. This labor of love is an example of the spirit of ASI!

"Scatter Like the Leaves of Autumn"

For many years, Mr. and Mrs. Gilbert Wilks cherished a desire to uplift the quality of life in the homes of America. Their story began almost twenty-five years ago when Gilbert was employed as the production manager for Christian Record Braille Foundation, Inc., in Lincoln, Nebraska. Gilbert and his wife, Myrna, wanted to do something for the Lord in the mission field.

An opening developed for a print shop manager at Enterprise Academy in Kansas. When they arrived to accept the position, Gilbert and Myrna found that the press was printing a TV schedule that included a few inspirational thoughts, for distribution in Abilene, Kansas—a city eight miles away. Gilbert began to add more positive reading material to the TV booklet, including a meditation for each week. The booklet reached people of all denominations and was called *Family Happiness*. The Wilkses decided that *Steps to Christ* should be offered free at the end of each meditation, and a follow-up letter invited readers to order free copies of *The Desire of Ages* and *The Great Controversy*.

In 1969, the Wilkses went into business for themselves, locating at Highland Academy in Portland, Tennessee. Circulation of the guide quickly grew, with 382,000 *Family Happiness* booklets available at 3,200 grocery and drug stores throughout America.

One day as I flew from Atlanta, Georgia, to Washington, D.C., who should walk on board but Gilbert. He carried a large envelope containing printing materials. Soon he was telling me about an idea he'd had to print *Steps to Christ* in a colorful, economical edition. Gilbert was on his way to the Review and Herald Publishing Association, who had agreed to print this special edition of *Steps to Christ*. The new edition would bear the name *Happiness Digest*. As a matter of fact, Gilbert and his family had moved out in faith and had spent $15,000 of their own money for the project. This was the first I had heard of this new venture.

Gilbert had already ordered 50,000 copies just to fill the requests on hand that had come in from *Family Happiness*. When he saw how well this new edition of *Steps to Christ* was being accepted, he spoke with the officers of a newly formed organization, ASI Missions, Inc. He was asked to bring 30,000 copies to the national ASI convention. There, these 30,000 copies were quickly purchased, and 25,000 more were ordered. It was my privilege to purchase the very first box of *Happiness Digest*.

The national ASI board of directors agreed on the project of mailing *Happiness Digest* to every home in America. At the national ASI convention in 1983, members donated $500,000 to be applied to the first two million books to be mailed out. Gilbert now estimates that over twelve million *Happiness Digest* books have been printed and circulated throughout the world.

As another family moved forward with the spirit of ASI, God's good news was being "scattered like the leaves of autumn."

8

Eighteen Wheels and the Gospel

Those participating in the evening service walked onto the platform. It was a Friday evening at the Southern Union ASI chapter meeting in Florida. I recognized everyone except a smiling gentleman whom I had not met. As introductions were made, Elder Maurice Abbott, the Southern Union ASI secretary, introduced the guest speaker, Gary Dunlap, who drives a big eighteen-wheel diesel truck all over the country. When the chairman mentioned Gary's name, a big, genuine, friendly smile spread across his face.

I settled back in my chair in the front row of seats. As Gary walked over to the lectern, he smiled again from ear to ear and began to tell us about Jesus. He commented on a Bible verse, then started talking about his conviction of sharing Jesus with those he met along the way. Within two or three minutes, I was on the edge of my chair. For the remainder of the evening, we were all spellbound. Everyone attending was deeply moved by his testimony.

After the meeting, I invited Gary to be one of our speakers at the national convention in the fall. We taped his talk, and a slightly edited transcription of it follows. From it, you can get an idea of Gary's exciting way of witnessing . . .

> Ye have not chosen me, but I have chosen you, and ordained you, that ye should go and bring forth fruit, and that your fruit should remain. John 15:16.

Praise God! We may not see immediate results from what we do, but one day we will. One day we'll have a person come up to us and say, "It was you who invited me here." Oh, to be used of God—that is my desire.

In Elijah's day, the Lord withheld the rain. There came a famine and a thirst in the land. Amos says that in the last days another famine is coming, but it won't be from lack of food or water. It says they will run to and fro over the earth, and from the east to the west, and the Word of God they shall not find. Could it be that we are living in that day? People are running in every direction looking for the Word of God—not just any word, but a "thus saith the Lord." They are looking for truth. I meet people everywhere who tell me they have been searching for years. I believe it is time we are about our Father's business.

About five years ago, I was in Raven, Virginia, and suddenly realized that my light was not shining as effectively as it might. I woke up that morning, and the Holy Spirit was close to me. I had a tear in my eye. I had a warmth about my heart that just drew me to the Lord. I said, "Oh, Lord, save me! Save me, but let me witness for You. I want to hear Your voice."

When we pass through the waters, He says, "I'll be with you." Oh, when I pass through the truck stops, when I go to restaurants or wherever I'm going, and through those dark nights of fog and rain and down those steep mountain grades, I want Jesus with me! But most of all, I want my life to be fruitful, and I need Jesus to be able to witness.

On this particular morning, I pulled into a rest area thirty miles up the road. I stood around for about five minutes and said, "Lord, surely among all these people there is one person to whom I can witness." I got into my truck, started the engine, and turned on the air conditioner. I looked to the right, and there was a man waving his hand at me. "Oh," I said, "Thank You, Lord!"

The man walked over and asked, "How are you, sir? My wife has always wanted to see inside one of these eighteen-wheelers. Could she get up in your truck and look it over?"

"Bring her over!" I said.

She came over, and they introduced themselves. His name was Clifford, and his wife's name was Ann. When she sat down on that air-cushioned seat, she bounced on it like a kid and really enjoyed it. When she had climbed down, I asked, "Where are you folks going, and where have you been? Have you been on vacation?"

"Yes," she replied, "we've been to Florida. We're going back home to Buffalo, New York."

"Bless your heart," I answered. "I know you have had a nice trip, but while you are riding along, how would you like to read a good book? Something that will make you a better person. Something that will give you some knowledge and will help you have more to live for."

"Oh, yes, we would," Ann responded.

Now, I stack all kinds of books in my truck: *The Great Controversy*, *The Desire of Ages*, *Steps to Christ*, *The Other Side of Death*, and some magazines. This time I pulled out *The Great Controversy*, climbed down from the truck, and handed it to them.

"Oh, Clifford!" Ann exclaimed to her husband, "I told you so. When that man walked by the car, I felt something! This book was taught to me as a child. I know Seventh-day Adventists. I know all about the Sabbath. I told you we shouldn't be going to church on Sunday. We ought to be going on God's holy Sabbath day."

"You're right, young lady," I agreed. "God sent me here with this book. I have been praying all the way up the road, 'Lord, send me to an honest heart. I need to witness. I need to let the water of life flow through me.' "

Ann asked me to explain to her husband about the Sabbath from my Bible. I explained the three angels' messages. Truly, this was a divine appointment!

I went on to Branford, Connecticut, to pick up a trailerload, but something had happened, and it wasn't loaded. I called my office, and the boss told me to get a motel room and wait for the load the next day at noon. I didn't wait until noon. I got there about nine o'clock. I saw a truck parked there from Napa Truck Lines. I was driving for Raylock, which is a division of Napa.

The driver of this truck was out of Columbus, Ohio. I had been praying, "Let me have a good experience today." I introduced myself to this man and found out his name was John. He was a nice fellow who smiled freely, but his eyes looked tired. He looked like a man who was not feeling well.

"John," I asked, "how's your health?"

"I just got out of the hospital," he replied. "I've been off work for three months or more recuperating."

I invited him to come outside where we could hear a little better, as the plant was very noisy. I saw an opportunity to witness.

"John," I asked, "are you a Christian? Do you know Christ?"

"Yes," he responded, "I just joined the Baptist church."

"Praise God," I said. "The Lord is leading in your life. Will you get in my truck and study the Bible? If you believe that all things work together for good to them that love God, I know you believe that He brought us together."

"Oh, my," John answered, "what a thrill to meet a man like you."

"No, it's not me, brother," I assured him. "I'm just another truck driver. I want you to meet Jesus, and while I am introducing you to Him, you can be introducing me to Him—it works both ways." What a beautiful experience we had in that truck!

As I began to turn the pages of my Bible, I felt impressed to give him a study on the Sabbath. But I don't point out only the Sabbath—every one of those Ten Commandments is important. I pointed out that we must love God with all our heart and love our neighbors as ourselves, and on these two commands hang all the law. I came to the Sabbath question and began, "Remember the Sabbath day to keep it holy. Six days shalt thou labor . . ."

"Gary," John said, "may I interrupt you? You know, I have been drinking and smoking. I've cursed and done everything contemptible. When I had this heart attack and was lying there in the hospital, I heard my wife outside the door talking to her pastor. She said, 'Whatever you do, don't mention religion! Why, he's liable to go into a rage and have another heart attack!' I was listening to every word they said, and I knew that I needed something that this man had.

"When that Baptist minister came into my room, he just couldn't hold back, and he began talking to me about Jesus."

Then John told me that before the pastor had even entered the room, he had prayed, "God, if you will let me live through this, whatever You want me to do, I will do it—just show it to me."

After John got out of the hospital, he joined the Baptist church. He began reading the Bible. Everything he read in the Bible led him to Jesus and the Ten Commandments. All through the Psalms, everything he read was, "My commandments, My commandments." The Sabbath seemed to make a real impression on him.

One day he said, "I've got to go and see that preacher." So he got his Bible and called his preacher and said, "Could

I come over and talk with you?" When he got to this minister's house, John asked him, "Why is it that we worship on a day called Sunday—the first day of the week—when the Bible doesn't mention it?"

Well, the Baptist minister started to tell him that the resurrection of Christ was the reason. When the minister finished, John thanked him. Now, as John told me about all this, he said, "Gary, I've been praying ever since that God would give me a better understanding of His Word. I know God put you and me together."

I said, "Amen, brother. I've been praying that God would lead me, and you are one of the sheep who hears His voice."

Tears began to stream down John's cheeks.

"I want to be a Seventh-day Adventist," he said. "You've convinced me right here that God has a commandment-keeping people, and I am going to be one of them." When he left me, tears were still streaming down his face. Another divine appointment.

Some time later, Elder Neal Wilson contacted our office asking for an ASI member who might speak at an annual colloquium for all the ministers at the General Conference. Gary Dunlap was the man for this appointment. The evening came, and Gary and his wife, Janet, arrived in their eighteen-wheeler.

"What shall I say to all of these ministers?" he asked me.

"Gary, talk to us the same way that you share with ASI members," I said.

The Holy Spirit was in Gary's presentation. At the close of his talk, there was not a dry eye in the room. During his presentation, Gary explained his Christian philosophy with this poem by Edgar Guest:

I don't know how to say it,
But somehow it seems to me
That maybe we are stationed

Where God wants us to be.

That the little place I'm filling
is the reason for my birth
And just to do that work I do,
He sent me down to earth.

If God had wanted otherwise,
I reckon He'd have made
me just a little different,
or a worse or better grade.

And since God knows and understands
all things of land and sea
I fancy that He placed me here
just where He wanted me.

Sometimes I get to thinking
as my labors I review
That I should like a higher place
with greater tasks to do,

But I come to the conclusion
when the envying is stilled,
That the post to which God sent me
is the post He wanted filled.

So I plod along and struggle
in the hope when day is through
That I'm really necessary to
the things God wants to do,

And there isn't any service
I can give that I should scorn
For it may be just the reason
God allowed me to be born.

9

"This Is Irene's Drive-in"

As you approach the window to order your lunch at Irene's place, you see Bible verses on the window, as well as the menu. Or you might read there a question about something in the Bible. If you know the answer, you will receive a free drink with your lunch.

All this takes place on old U.S. Route 66, at the corner of Broadway and "D" Streets, in Needles, California. A few years ago, Irene's place was "business as usual." Then something happened that turned Irene's place into "business as unusual!"

I spoke in the Needles church in 1969, when there were only twenty-two very quiet members. The next year, the Les Brian family moved to a small town, Essex, forty-one miles west of Needles. They were new members of the Adventist faith. Les told me he thought the Needles church needed some help. I encouraged him to go door-to-door and invite people to attend his Bible class. Many people came to the classes, and they showed a strong interest in spiritual things.

Les then came to my office and asked what he should do next. The time for reaping had obviously arrived, and an evangelist came to Needles and conducted meetings. Twenty-two people received the Lord Jesus and were baptized. The membership in the Needles church had doubled in a relatively short time.

Seeing all of these good things happening, Irene Kernigan began to get up about four in the morning for Bible study and prayer. This time of communion with the Lord resulted in a spiritual renewal in her life. Then God began to use her.

As Irene sat under the hair dryer at the beauty parlor one day, she busied herself cutting out felts to use in the children's Sabbath School class. Some of the ladies there asked what she was doing. One of the beauty operators told Irene that she and her husband had been visiting various churches but had not found answers to their questions.

"Irene," she asked, "would you came out to our home to study the Bible with us?"

Irene and Louise Kernigan went to the Gene Disney home to hold the requested Bible studies. They found several others who also had Bible questions. The first thing the people asked was, "What is the mark of the beast?"

In this study group were several younger men and their families—men who worked for the railroad. The studies continued, and interest in the Word of God deepened. Later, an evangelist was holding meetings in Kingman, Arizona, sixty-five miles east of Needles. The Bible study group attended those meetings each night. When the crusade was finished, twenty-eight more people were baptized on one Sabbath and joined the Needles church.

Irene's Drive-in has had a great impact on the Needles community. She is a happy, positive, friendly Christian who loves everyone. When people come to the window to order their food, they are greeted by a big smile and asked, "What are you going to have, darlin'?" In the lonely world we live in, many of those customers may be coming to the drive-in as much to be called "darlin'" as to order a taco. What a positive influence in this troubled world—to have a Seventh-day Adventist Christian share a kind word or a smile—or talk to people about Jesus!

One of Irene's customers wrote a poem about her and her work as he was eating his lunch:

Irene's Place

Away out in the desert
Away from the river apace
There is a little eating joint
By the name of "Irene's Place."
Irene is a friendly one
And is never hard nor terse,
Before you get any food
You must quote a Bible verse.
She always lends a helping hand
To the hungry and the poor,
And if you need food for thought
Hers is an open door.
The place is a monument
to God's goodness and His love,
She is as wise as a serpent
And as harmless as a dove.
Out there in lonesome Needles
Away from the city's bang,
She'll fill your empty stomach
With a Chitti Bang Bang!
Here's an ode to sweet Irene
And her happy eating place,
May she always have God's blessing
And most of all, His grace.

Gerry Guernsey, M.D.
December 17, 1980

Not surprisingly, with this witness—felt by an entire city—the Needles church outgrew its house of worship. In 1990, ASI Mission Church Builders constructed a new 250-seat sanctuary for the congregation, a fellowship hall, and a church school adequate for the church's growing needs. Recently, another evangelistic series was conducted, and twenty more persons were baptized. The membership of the church as this book is written is 170.

Needles is a desert town of 4,700 plus, located on the Colorado River near the California-Arizona state border. The Santa Fe Railroad has its switching facility in the town. Most people would tell you that a town like Needles fits the formula for a non-growth church. But the members of the Needles church didn't know this. They are a loving, friendly, kind group of Christians who welcome you warmly as you enter the sanctuary for worship.

In this lovely new place of worship there is no expensive organ. Instead, you may hear some happy, smiling worshipers singing and playing the guitar. They believe that their purpose in life is to invite both friends and strangers to prepare to meet Jesus very soon!

Irene has spoken all over the United States for Adventist and other denominational church functions, including camp meetings, seminars, and ASI conventions. She is booked well in advance to share her witness. Irene was one of the speakers who shared her testimony at the last two General Conference sessions in 1985 and 1990.

Another ASI member, sharing the missionary spirit!

10

The Hall of Fame

What do a promise in the cornfield, a mechanic, and a smuggler have to do with ASI? From time to time, ASI has honored those members in the organization who have not knowingly sought recognition but who have unselfishly gone beyond the call of duty to serve God and humanity. These are Christian men and women who have worked untiringly "to do justly, and to love mercy, and to walk humbly with thy God." Micah 6:8.

ASI leaders decided that those members who had engaged in their various ministries for at least twenty-five years and had made singular contributions in witnessing should be honored. These would have to be members who were a proven credit to their church and community—and effective witnesses for their Lord. At the 1983, 1984, and 1985 national ASI conventions, honors were presented to Dr. Chessie Harris, Dr. Marion Barnard, and Dr. John H. Weidner, respectively.

It was on one of those lovely mornings on the island of Kauai, Hawaii, at an ASI national convention, that I first heard Mrs. Chessie Harris speak. This gentle, humble lady began describing the beginnings of the Harris Home for Children. I sensed that this woman was an extraordinary person. From her very first words, it was apparent that she was well acquainted with the Almighty.

Chessie described the living conditions in which she found the children of the Huntsville, Alabama, area where she lived. She and George, her husband, began to take girls and boys into their own home and to care for them. She said that they took only those children who had been rejected by parents or other agencies. The God of heaven, she said, had been their sponsor. Miracles of every description had occurred on behalf of their work in providing for these boys and girls.

Words cannot describe how my soul was touched by the loving family of Chessie and George Harris.

Once an agency called the Harris Home asking Chessie to care for three children on a temporary basis. The mother was using the children for income, and for this reason, they were being removed from their terrible situation. All three of them were greatly frightened to be taken from their home.

Chessie held one of the little girls close as she rocked her in her chair. Chessie said she could feel the child's heart pounding against her breast as she comforted her. Stories like this about her love and concern for hurting children could fill a book. Getting acquainted with a family like the Harrises is one of those rare experiences a person might have once in a lifetime.

In January 1982, I had the privilege of visiting the Harris Home for Children. When the boys and girls posed for a picture with Chessie, every single child wanted to touch her. She was the object of the same respect and love that each child had experienced in the Harris Home for Children.

During the 1983 ASI national convention held at Lake Guntersville, Alabama, we felt that this Christian service, as demonstrated to humanity by the Harris family, should be recognized. Chessie had been having some difficulty with her heart, and we were concerned that this might be too much for her at the time. I was able to get her husband aside to learn if we should go ahead with the awards. He looked me in the eye and said,"She'll be all right for this."

Chessie was invited to tell about her mission in life after the Sabbath School lesson study. We had made a special plaque called the ASI Christian Service Award to be presented to Chessie on this occasion. The president of the United States, Ronald Reagan, sent a citation to Chessie honoring her for her twenty-nine years of caring and loving service to children. At the time of the convention, she said that over the years she and her husband had cared for 831 children needing love and care. This was in 1983—and the Harris Home continues to serve!

These honors came as a surprise to Chessie. She had no inkling that the ASI had chosen to recognize her work in this way. When the presentations were made, Chessie was so surprised that she began to shed tears of joy and appreciation. The 550 people in attendance gave her a lengthy standing ovation. There was not a dry eye in the audience that Sabbath morning.

For some time I felt that the story of the Harris family needed to be told. First of all, they needed to be recognized by their church, and second, the story needed to be told as an encouragement to others to take homeless children into their homes. Now a detailed account of the Harris family's work can be read in the book *Promise in the Cornfield*, written by Madlyn Hamblin and published in 1989.

Since then, Chessie has appeared on many television programs to tell her story. This is the kind of positive story Americans need to hear. A while back, I called to talk to Chessie, but she was not home. Her daughter said, "She is speaking at the high school graduation this evening."

Chessie returned the call and told us that Andrews University would soon be conferring on her a Doctorate of Humanities degree. In 1989, she was invited by President George Bush to be one of eighteen honored volunteers in the United States to come to the White House for recognition. She sat next to the president that evening at the special White House banquet. Congratulations, Dr. Chessie Harris! You have always had a beautiful spirit!

★★★★

In 1962, I attended a meeting in Los Angeles where Dr. Marion C. Barnard, a physician and surgeon, from Bakersfield, California, was the featured speaker. As I listened to this Christian gentleman, I became aware that he was a man of vision for God and humanity—a man with a mission. After the meeting, I talked to Dr. Barnard about his zest for bringing people to Christ.

"Who instilled this soul-winning desire in you," I asked. "Your father or mother?"

"No," he answered. "When I was a young man, I worked in an auto repair garage, and the owner would talk to his customers about Christ and give them Bible studies. He brought many people to the Lord by his outreach."

After Dr. Barnard graduated from La Sierra Junior College, he became an automobile mechanic. He and his new bride, Cleo Pauline Fenderson, looked for the state that had the fewest number of Adventists. So the Barnards moved to Arkansas, where he went to work as a mechanic.

After some time, the Barnards moved back to California, where he became the business manager for a medical group in Fullerton. It was there that he realized the wonderful opportunity a doctor had to witness to people. He returned to La Sierra College to take pre-med and graduated with the class of 1944 from the College of Medical Evangelists—now called Loma Linda University.

"This missionary work appealed to me," he told me, "and I thought that a doctor had one of the best opportunities to talk to people about Jesus."

Some time ago, I was in his office in Bakersfield, and I

noticed that the reading material in the waiting room was made up entirely of religious books and journals. He said, "You can find secular magazines anywhere."

Many of his patients read the literature while waiting, and by the time they enter the doctor's office, they have questions. This opens the door for him to talk to them about the Great Physician. For several years, Dr. and Mrs. Barnard have invited patients to their home for a Bible class. Those who have come to the class have been invited to attend his Sabbath School class. Several hundred people have received the Lord and become Adventist Christians because of his ministry.

In a letter I received from his daughter, Dr. Jo Ellen Barnard Walton, she writes, "Daddy has always had a very special interest in mission work. He has contributed heavily to missions around the world and has made trips to the hospitals in the South Pacific Division." Dr. Barnard made trips to Africa and Ethiopia to relieve some doctors that they might have some rest. He also gave volunteer help at the Banipa, Nepal hospital, Karachi, Pakistan, and Kerala, India.

A full-page story in the Bakersfield *Californian* on April 1, 1984 announced: "A surprise dinner, with over 1500 people present, was given to honor Dr. Barnard on his 75th birthday and for over 40 years of medical practice."

The paper then went on to detail Dr. Barnard's work in their city. "As a public servant, he is chairman of the board of San Joaquin Community Hospital, chairman of the board of the American Red Cross chapter, as well as other programs such as 'Heartbeat,' which is a low-cost coronary screening program designed to help people to avoid heart attacks. But perhaps his best known interest is in helping underdeveloped, third-world countries as a Seventh-day Adventist layman, donating his time to medical missions. Once or twice each year, he and his family (often accompanied by other volunteers) travel to such areas as New Guinea, Solomon Islands and Vanuatu to provide medical help for the native people who otherwise would not have any hope of a cure."

"It is not a sacrifice to do this," Dr. Barnard says. "The trips are great fun, and the best pay a doctor could hope to get is a shell or carving brought by a patient who has no money and whose only real means of payment is love."

At one public gathering to honor Dr. Barnard, telephone calls and personal greetings were received from persons in the areas where he had worked. Over $55,000 was donated by guests who wished to help him construct medical clinics in places that do not presently have medical help. I am told that many of those who attended this gathering asked if they could come to be in the Bible class that meets in his home. The number of requests was more than he could accommodate, so some had to be put on a waiting list. Dr. Barnard has helped other physicians develop programs and Bible studies for witnessing through their offices.

Dr. Marion Barnard rightly deserved the ASI Christian Service Award and a citation from President Ronald Reagan. Dr. Marion has always brought Christian service and the spirit of ASI into our conventions!

★★★★

One of the most dedicated Christian businessmen you will ever meet is Dr. John H. Weidner. His Christian service began as a Seventh-day Adventist during World War II. John is of Dutch descent—the son of an Adventist minister who served pastorates in Holland, Belgium, Switzerland, and France. He studied at the Seminaire Adventiste at Collonges, France, and graduated in theology, classics, and business. He continued his graduate studies in law and business at the University of Geneva and later in Paris. Following his studies, he entered the import-export business in Paris.

During World War II, the Nazis invaded Holland and then reached Paris. John tried to reach England to join the

Allied armies but was unsuccessful. Instead, he stayed in Lyons, France, to help many of the refugees with an escape line through Holland, Belgium, and France to the free countries of Switzerland and Spain. More than 1,000 refugees—among them Jewish people, Allied airmen, Catholic priests, and political refugees—were helped through this line of safety.

John Weidner was arrested several times but successfully escaped each time, even though a high price was placed on his head. He was one of the German Gestapo's most-wanted men. He worked closely with Dr. W.A. Visser't Hooft, General Secretary of the World Council of Churches, to help the refugees and bring messages from Geneva to World Council member churches of the occupied countries. This courier line also helped bring news from the Allied command to the underground of the occupied countries, and vice versa. More than 300 people were used in this organization, called Dutch Paris. Many members of this group dedicated to helping others were arrested, and forty died in concentration camps, among them John's own sister.

After the war, several of the Allied governments decorated John. President Harry Truman honored him with the Medal of Freedom; King George VI conferred on John the Military Order of the British Empire; Queen Wilhelmina from Holland, the Order of Orange-Nassau; the French government, the Legion of Honor, the Croix le Guerre, and the French Medaille de la Resistance. He was honored by the City of Hope in 1986 as Man of the Year, and he has been honored with many other awards from several organizations.

The government of Israel honored Weidner by entering his name among those of the heroes in the Golden Book of Jerusalem, by planting a tree in his honor in the Alley of the Righteous Gentile in Yad Washem in Jerusalem, and by awarding him the Medal of the Righteous Gentile.

After the war, John was asked by the Dutch government

to enter diplomatic service to help the Minister of Justice in the prosecution of war criminals. He stayed in the diplomatic service of the Dutch embassy in Paris and traveled throughout Europe in this capacity.

In 1950, John asked the government to relieve him from his duties, as he felt that his task was fulfilled. In 1955, he came to the United States, where he met and married Naomi Browalsky, a registered nurse from the White Memorial Hospital. Today John and Naomi Weidner live in southern California. John is president of a corporation that manufactures vitamins and owns a chain of health food stores.

Beyond all these well-earned honors, the Weidners are leaders in their church. John has served as head elder of the Pasadena SDA Church, as a member of the executive committee of the Southern California Conference, as an executive board member of the Media Center of the General Conference, and as the first treasurer of the premiere ASI chapter to be formed, in the Pacific Union. He has also served his community as president of the Chamber of Commerce, Rotary Club, and other organizations.

Besides all of their civic speaking appointments and church activities, John and Naomi are invited year after year to speak at many synagogues and Jewish organizations about John's activities to aid Jewish people during World War II.

On May 17, 1992, on its 105th anniversary, Atlantic Union College of South Lancaster, Massachusetts, honored John Weidner by conferring on him the degree of Doctor of Laws *in honoris causa.* The college will build a multimillion-dollar "Weidner Center" for the study of altruism.

But perhaps most important of all in John's career is his unfailing interest in the spirituality of his customers and his employees. Approximately forty people with whom the Weidners have studied and worked have become Adventist Christians.

One example is John's secretary, Vicki. She became

interested in the Bible because of the worship period John and Naomi held in the store each day for their employees. Vicki became an Adventist and witnessed to her two sisters, who also became Adventist Christians. Other members of Vicki's family, too, became Adventists.

The Weidners have become role models for other ASI members in reaching out to their community and preparing people for eternity. When I presented the ASI Christian Service Award to John Weidner at the 1985 national ASI convention, he said, "This is the greatest honor that has been given to me, because it is from my church!" President Ronald Reagan sent to John a citation from the White House along with his congratulations. The Weidner family always brings the ASI spirit into our conventions!

11

ASI Members Behind Bars

If you really believe the world needs to hear that Jesus is coming soon, why don't you spend all your time telling everybody?" the businessman asked unexpectedly. It was many years ago when Richard Bland heard this—the greatest challenge of his life—while serving on an advisory board for the President of the United States. The question penetrated to the depth of Richard's soul for several years.

Aware that they were witnessing the closing scenes of the world's history, Mr. and Mrs. Richard A. Bland left their successful real estate and banking business in California and moved to Birmingham, Alabama, to open a vegetarian restaurant. During the time the Blands were planning their move, they were invited to visit a prison one afternoon. Providentially, the scheduled speaker did not arrive, and as Richard spoke to these men, the Holy Spirit convicted his heart that here were souls hungering and thirsting for truth. This was the beginning of something no one could have foreseen.

Under the Lord's direction, Richard took 200 paperback books to give to the prisoners. One day the prison chaplain requested an additional 1,000 of "those beautiful books by E. G. White." This positive response to the books prompted the Blands to make up a packet of books and literature for the inmates, including such titles as *What the Bible Says*, *Bible Readings for the Home*, *Steps to Christ*, and *100 Facts on the Bible Sabbath*.

Richard then organized a small group that made visits to the prison for religious services. The original board of directors of this group consisted of Richard Bland, Cris Davis, and Robert Santini—at that time president of Pine Hill Sanitarium.

They sensed that the inmates were more receptive to small Bible-study groups than to preaching. The Lord directed them to devise a set of simple but potent Bible studies called "What the Bible Says." Bland's group trained prisoners to be leaders of their own Bible classes after they had first successfully completed the Bible course and had enrolled at least three inmates.

For the first three years, the Blands used their own funds to supply literature for the inmates, but the demand was greater than one family could handle financially. So an appeal for more volunteers to help in the prison ministry went out to thirteen local Adventist churches. Within a short time, 104 volunteers were grading 1,600 Bible lessons each week. This was the beginning—in 1981—of United Prison Ministries.

"Praise the Lord! Thank You, Jesus! If the Bible says it, I'll believe it. If God commands it, I will do it. If it's good enough for Jesus, it's good enough for me!" chants a room full of white-garbed prisoners, guards, and Seventh-day Adventist laymen. This is a familiar scene at United Prison Ministries meetings.

"If you don't have a Bible text for it, we don't talk about it," Bland says.

When some of the inmates were transferred to other

prisons, they asked for UPM to come into those prisons. UPM visits only the prisons that invite them to come in with their program. United Prison Ministries has been exceptionally well received by prison administrations because of the lasting effect on the inmates. In a letter to Bland dated May 19, 1983, the outgoing commander of the Birmingham City Jail, Carl V. Garrett, wrote:

> I have been a police officer for 30 years and have never known of a more effective program than United Prison Ministries. I have told Mr. Alexander [his successor] that if the number of groups coming in is cut down to one, you should be the one to continue . . . If people could just realize that every inmate that you cause to change is one less threat to our safety at home, in our businesses, and on the streets, they would give [to support UPM] out of pure selfishness.[1]

In an official proclamation, Birmingham, Alabama, Mayor Richard Arrington, Jr., declared September 10, 1983, "Prison Ministry Day" in honor of UPM's work.

Speaking of UPM's mission, Richard Bland states:

> It is our mission to provide prisoners with an opportunity to receive the gospel message by providing spiritual material to them. The prisoners can use the time they have been given to learn about Christ. The choice is theirs. By providing them with spiritual food, the Holy Spirit will be able to convince many hearts.[2]

And according to the UPM newsletter:

> United Prison Ministries is currently involved in over 600 prisons in all 50 states and Canada and several foreign countries including Africa, Australia, Canada, England, France, Norway and Russia.[3]

In 1989, United Prison Ministries became United Prison Ministries, International. It has distributed over 8.2 million pieces of literature, including Bibles, Bible lessons, and Spirit of Prophecy books. Included in this statistic are seven million Bible lessons recently sent to Russia.

The chief of the prison in the Ukraine asked Richard personally to send 700,000 Bibles for the inmates in his prisons. He said, "We do not have trouble with the prisoners who read the Bible." No report can be accurate as to those who have received Christ and become members of the Adventist church because of this fast-moving evangelistic thrust to such a captive audience. UPMI also uses the Bible lessons for the families of the inmates. Many of the wives and children of the prisoners have been baptized.

Following are a couple of typical testimonies that have appeared in the UPMI *Insider's Report*:[4]

"My two sons were brought up in a Seventh-day Adventist home; now both of them are in prison. They met United Prison Ministries while there and now they are both back on track with Jesus. Praise the Lord for UPM," states a happy mother in New York.

"I want to be baptized and join the SDA church. Please help me know more about Jesus. I want to dedicate my life to Him," says Thomas, a prisoner in Soledad, California.

UPMI—taking the ASI spirit behind bars!

Notes:

1. Gary L. Ivey, as quoted in *Southern Tidings*, January 1984, pp. 2, 3.
2. As quoted by Natalie C. Hardin, *Self-Supporting Worker*, July 1990, p. 14.
3. United Prison Ministries International *Insider's Report*, 1992.
4. Ibid.

12

God Pursues a Physician

The gentleman conducting the Sabbath School lesson at the 1989 national ASI convention spoke with obvious enthusiasm and conviction. I still haven't forgotten his presentation.

Dr. Willard D. Regester was excited about the Lord and was doing something about it in his life. I have been following his outreach and some of the things he has been doing for some time. When I read about his idea of the Aaron and Hur Club, I thought there should be a chapter in this book about his witness and testimony! Here is another ASI member showing the ASI spirit! The remainder of this chapter is his own story, as he shared it with me:

There I was, on the tenth floor of the Guest Quarters hotel in Atlanta, Georgia, with one end of a rope tied around my ankle and the other securely tied to the leg of the bed. Locked in a titanic negotiating session with the Holy Spirit, I was fearful I might jump to end my life and thereby avoid a life-and-death struggle—a struggle in which I sought either to retain some of my cherished sins and yet be saved, or to yield fully to the Holy Spirit. And the Spirit continued to say, "All or nothing at all." This was Wednesday, June 19, 1985. But wait—I'm getting ahead of my story.

Back in early August of 1981, as I drove to a restaurant to have lunch with a colleague, I pondered the past few months of my medical practice. Those months had been far too busy, and I was not only burned out, I was melted down. I was just plain tired of seeing patients. So as I neared the restaurant, I decided to ask my doctor friend if he would like to buy my practice. As I was eating the salad, I posed the question to him, and before we had eaten the dessert, the whole deal had been consummated and the details written out on a table napkin. I returned to my office and announced the sale.

Retirement? Never! Within a week I had landed a job with Technicon Corporation, a subsidiary of Revlon, and after a two-week vacation with my wife in New Zealand, Australia, and Fiji, I started my new career. From the start it was interesting, exciting, and challenging. After three years with Technicon I was placed in charge of expanding our sales into overseas markets. During 1984 and early 1985 I crossed the Atlantic nine times.

Yes, I was in the fast lane, and I loved it. Yet my life at home and abroad was not that of a Christian, and the Holy Spirit continued to make me aware of that fact. The Holy Spirit's pursuit intensified, and I am absolutely convinced that God the Father said to God the Holy Spirit, "Let's mount one more offensive and see if we can capture that sinner Regester."

That offensive began on the evening of May 23, 1985, in New York City. I had just finished showing a group from Germany some of Technicon's east coast installations and finished off with dinner at the Windows of the World restaurant atop the World Trade Center. Having bade them good-bye, I walked the streets of New York before retiring to my hotel.

About then, I realized something strange was going on. I couldn't identify the problem, but over the course of the next few weeks the power of God invaded my very being, leading soon to the scene in Atlanta I described earlier.

On May 24, I flew home to Saratoga, California, and as the days passed rapidly, so also the intensity of the Holy Spirit's offensive increased rapidly. Incredible as it may seem, I had not yet figured out what was going on. I did not yet realize that the battle for my soul was under way. What I did know was that I could not sleep at night. I could not pour milk out of a carton without spilling it, and my power of concentration was markedly compromised.

Finally, on Saturday night, June 15, it began to dawn on me that I had to change my lifestyle. I had to get things right with my wife. So after several hours on my knees, the agonizing hours of confession began and went on through the wee hours of the morning. Sunday passed fitfully, and on Monday I flew to Texas to make a presentation at Baylor University. After the presentation, I flew on to Atlanta, Georgia—headquarters for Technicon—arriving at Guest Quarters at 2 a.m. on Tuesday. It was in my room here that the final scenes of the battle raged.

Unbelievable as it may seem, in retrospect, I had not yet grasped that I was in the midst of a "traumatic conversion." Since the experiences of the next three days would fill a book—a luxury I do not have—let me simply describe a few of the highlights.

I had not one moment of sleep from Tuesday morning until 2:30 a. m. Friday. All night Tuesday, I was on my knees with a Bible in hand, pleading my case before God. I was willing to lay aside *some* sins—but some were just too "good" to let go!

Wednesday night I felt I might jump from the tenth floor so as to escape the inevitable—total capitulation. This fear drove me to tie myself to the bed. Wednesday evening—again all night on my knees—I surrendered a few more of my pet sins, but the Holy Spirit is a very one-sided negotiator. He insists on total surrender.

If you would like to read an exact description of my physical body at this juncture, just read Psalm 22:14, 15. Just when I thought I would die, the Holy Spirit led me to this passage. How I praise Him! Thursday night crept into Friday morning, and at 1:30 a.m., I capitulated. I finally said, "OK, God, I give up. Give me the strength to live for You, *BUT USE ME.*"

At 1:55 a.m. He touched me—the final event of that month-long pursuit—and in so doing said in essence, "OK, it's a deal. Live for me, and I will use you." This is the first time I have written the story of those eventful days, and in doing so, I again praise God for how He has led me in the past.

This story of my conversion is the answer to a question I am frequently asked: "Dr. Regester, what got you into doing these seminars?" But things do not always flow as easily or smoothly as a written recounting of events may make it appear. So it was in my case.

After that fateful Friday, I flew back to Saratoga, California, and began an intensive examination of my life. Wrongs had to be made right. Bridges had to be rebuilt. And then, of course, I had to seek an answer to the question, "OK now, Lord—what do You want me to do?"

In order to get that question answered, I had to implement a new set of habits. First, I called Technicon and resigned my position. I then established some absolutes: absolutely no television, absolutely no less than two hours of prayer and study morning and evening, and an end to all negative acquaintances and activities.

These were great resolutions, but inadequate in God's sight. As it turned out, during the following twelve months, He knew I needed more intensive training than that and thus led me to twelve to fifteen hours of prayer and study daily, during which time I read seventy-five books. Many of these books would be no surprise: the Bible, the Conflict of the Ages series, other Ellen White books. But I was also directed to many others by my best friend Raoul Dederen, then Dean of our seminary at Andrews University.

Prayer and study were great and absolutely necessary, but I must admit that as the first year rolled by, I was becoming impatient. According to my timetable, it was time for the Lord to act and get me into His work. He acted, but not as I had anticipated. Isn't that just like God?

Instead of giving me a preaching job, He knew I must start again to make a living, so through a combination of several distinct miracles, He led me back to that which was totally unthinkable. After having been absent from it for five years, He led me back into the practice of medicine. So now prayer, theological study, medical study, and my practice began to function in parallel, but still no answer came from the Lord as to the real task He wanted me to do.

After reopening my practice (another story that would need its own book!) it would be an understatement to say that time seemed to fly even faster just by virtue of the added activities. But one day in May 1989, I almost impulsively blurted out to my wife, "I think I'll start doing seminars." Finally, God had identified the task He had in mind.

So I began conducting Daniel and Revelation seminars. But I had never done anything like this before. So I called my friend, Raoul Dederen, and asked, "What do I do now?" He put me in touch with Russell Burrill, who heads up the North American Division evangelistic center. Russell literally walked and talked me through my first seminar.

I mention this to show that *anyone who wants to do God's work can do it!* He will give you the help you need. The stories I'm about to share with you bear out the fact that "We can do nothing of ourselves, but we can do all things through Jesus Christ who strengthens us." I am convinced that it is a rare person who cannot actively present Jesus Christ to the world. We need only to plug in to the Power. It is my sincere hope that as you read in the remainder of this chapter about God's miraculous workings, you too will be inspired to get involved with God—that you too will be infected with the excitement and fun of doing His work.

We held our first seminar in a Howard Johnson motel in the fall of 1989. Sixty-two people attended the first night. We were off and running. During this seminar, a 7.0 earthquake hit the San Francisco area. We missed only one night, and at the end of the seminar, the Lord gave us ten souls. I could hardly believe that God had used the efforts of just a few of us to garner in ten souls.

During the seminar, an attendee named Chris came to me and said, "Dr. Regester, I like what you have been saying the last few nights, and I believe you should be on television." I just laughed, but a couple of nights later she brought an application blank from a local TV station. I wrote down the following: "I teach end time events from the books of Daniel and Revelation"—and handed it back to her. She took it to the TV station.

I never saw Chris again, but eighteen months later I received a call from the station.

"Dr. Regester," the manager said, "in view of what is going on in the Persian Gulf, I think you should be on TV. We've had this application gathering dust around here, so come on down, and let's talk it over."

I have now been on this station over eighteen months. As I frequently say, "I'm no George Vandeman," yet I hope to meet souls on the other shore who were introduced to Jesus through this program.

Oh, yes, about Chris. I said I never saw her again. Never, that is, until two years later, when she came walking into my sixth seminar. One evening after the meeting, she said, "I've been watching you on television, and I want to help you with the expenses. She handed me an envelope containing $2,500. As this seminar came to an end, she, along with fourteen others, were baptized into God's remnant church. The mighty arm of God works!

A beautiful new hospital in San Jose was the site of our second seminar. Among the 180 people who came were Linda and Earl. They were regular "church-going people," but as I listened to their story, I could tell they bounced from church to church. They never missed a night at the seminar—until I presented the Sabbath, that is.

They had always attended with another couple—Bill and Betty. When Linda and Earl dropped out, as my custom was, I sat down to call them, but they had not provided a phone number. So I decided to write them—but they had also provided no address.

We had learned that they lived in Santa Clara, the next city north of San Jose. So I decided to write them, using what information I had, and let the Lord do the rest. My wife chided me a little when she saw me drop the letter in the mail, addressed to "Linda and Earl Smith, only God knows the street and house number, Santa Clara, California."

When Betty and Bill came the following Sunday evening, I could tell they were excited, and at the first opportunity they came running up to me and said, "They got the letter!" Again, God's mighty arm at work. He always does His part. How about us?

Allow me to share one of Ellen White's visions which haunted me and literally drove me to do a seminar for the professionals and affluent of Santa Clara County:

> Last night a scene was presented before me. I may never feel free to reveal all of it, but I will reveal a little. It seemed that an immense ball of fire came down upon the world, and crushed large houses. From place to place rose the cry, "The Lord has come! The Lord has come!" Many were unprepared to meet Him, but a few were saying, "Praise the Lord!" "Why are you praising the Lord?" inquired those upon whom was coming destruc-

> tion. "Because we now see what we have been looking for." "If you believed that these things were coming, why did you not tell us?" was the terrible response. "We did not know about these things. Why did you leave us in ignorance? Again and again you have seen us; why did you not become acquainted with us, and tell us of the judgment to come, and that we must serve God lest we perish? Now we are lost!" Every church member is to train the intellect, in order that he may gain a clear understanding of the will of God concerning him; everyone is to educate the voice, that he may communicate a knowledge of the Scriptures to those who are in ignorance. May God help us to stand, like Daniel, in our lot and place during the days of probation that remain.[1]

As I read and reread this vision, I would ask myself, "Have you invited your colleagues to hear the three angels' messages? Have you invited the attorneys of the area? How about the ministers of other persuasions?"

The answer was No to all these queries, so I was impressed to do a seminar for this group at the San Jose Radisson hotel. We sent out 50,000 invitations by name, and forty-six people came. Sharon was among those who attended. After the first evening's presentation, she came to me and said, "Let me tell you my story. I am a legal secretary, and I open my boss's mail. When I opened your invitation, I was delighted to see you were teaching Daniel. I have never been able to understand Daniel, but as I was praising God silently, the next paragraph of your letter stated that the cost of the seminar was $95." (We never charge for seminars, but for this select group, we did.)

Sharon said, "God, if you want me to go, you need to provide the $95." Within ten minutes after making this commitment, the phone rang. It was a local radio station calling with a quiz question worth $105. You guessed it. She paid the $95 with the prize money and had $10 left over for tithe. Does God work? Would you say it is exciting to be involved in these miracles? Believe me, it is!

Now, before I share further, let me ask you a question. Have you invited your hair dresser, your barber, your mechanic, the person at the check-out counter, your neighbor, or your friends at work to accept the Lord Jesus Christ? Have you introduced them to the message of the three angels? Where will you stand when these people say to you, "If you believed these things were coming, why did you not tell us?"

One day Mei and her husband, Jerry—a delightful Oriental couple—came to my office. She was active in the Catholic church, and he was a nonbeliever. This was the fall of 1991, and I handed her a flyer announcing the seminar to start in a couple of weeks.

"Mei," I invited, "come study with us. It will change your life."

She came; she studied. Frequently she asked for additional studies at the office. She was a real seeker for truth. Three months later she was baptized, along with several of the other seminar students. But that is not the end of the story. Mei started coming to the studio to help with the TV show. Her husband became interested, and a few days after Mei was baptized, he gave us a check for $2,000 to support the TV ministry for one year. Miracles, miracles, miracles! In God 's work, they never end.

I have always kept the seminars closely connected with the church. The local conference, our church, and some classmates and friends—along with my wife and I—have supported the seminars financially. At first the team consisted of about eight persons, but as baptisms have occurred, we immediately get these new people into the work. So now the team is about thirty strong, made up largely of new members. My office is enhanced by this activity. In fact, one assistant came to work for me who did not believe in God. He was baptized eighteen months later. He is now an active witness in the office and a worker in the church. Yes, the work is enjoyable and fulfilling, but it has not always been easy. Let me explain.

As I became increasingly active for the Lord, many people in the churches in the area became very nervous. Soon letters began coming to me and also started flying to the Central California Conference office. I took a heavy barrage of flack. Not because of *what* I was teaching—for it is conservative Adventism—but simply *because* I was teaching.

I determined to continue doing God's work, but while weathering the storm, I had occasion to speak to Elder Alfred McClure, president of the North American Division. I shared with him some of the problems. As we shared our thoughts, I came to realize that leaders as well as laity have similar problems.

One morning, shortly after my meeting with Elder McClure, I was on my knees praying, and Aaron and Hur came to my mind. I was dumfounded. Why was I thinking of Aaron and Hur? As I pondered that strange thought during that day, I was impressed to initiate an Aaron and Hur Club, with the express purpose of mobilizing the laity to hold high the hands of our leaders. It is time that criticism stop, and we spend our time witnessing for our Lord.

As I bring my personal experience to a close, you may be wondering how I got involved with ASI. Here again, I believe it was the leading of the Lord. A faithful ASI member, Dottie Davidson, visited my church and sat in my Sabbath School class. She told me she was going to try to get ASI to invite me to teach the Sabbath School lesson at its national convention in Hawaii.

She did, and I did. I liked the dedicated people I saw and liked even more what I saw them doing. I decided then and there to join ASI. Incidentally, the title for my Sabbath School presentation at the convention was "The Call, the Task, the Power." Responding to that title will always be my aim!

Notes:

1. Ms. 102, 1904.

13

Outpost Centers, Inc.

Outpost Centers, Inc. is a relatively new concept in lay ministry. Its parent institution—Wildwood Sanitarium and Medical Missionary Institute—dates back to the beginning of World War II.

In the fall of 1941, Neil Martin was searching for property on which to establish a rural sanitarium and medical missionary institute for the training of lay workers. He hoped that W.D. Frazee and George McClure would join him in the establishment of the institution.

Just outside Chattanooga, Tennessee, the old car Brother Martin was driving blew a gasket. While it was being repaired, he dropped in to see Dr. O.M. Hayward, a Seventh-day Adventist physician practicing in the city. His office happened to be across the street from where the car was being repaired.

"What are you doing here?" the kindly doctor queried.

"I am searching for a site on which to do the work Ellen White instructed God's people to do," Brother Martin replied.

"You know that the servant of the Lord has told us that the cities should be worked from an outpost," he continued. "She says in *Medical Ministry*, page 308 that it would be well to secure a place as a home for our mission workers outside of the city."

"Then I believe your search is over," the doctor replied with enthusiasm. "I think I have exactly what you are looking for. I would like for you to have a look at the farm I have out here in the country a ways."

So "out in the country a ways" the two men went—ten miles, in fact, northwest of Chattanooga. Here, Dr. Hayward's 500-acre farm, nestled in the low hills of north Georgia and Tennessee, seemed to be just waiting to become the site for the very dream the men had in mind. Here the mountainous wooded area sweeps up to the top of Raccoon Mountain in Tennessee. The whole campus faces historic Lookout Mountain, and the area within a twenty-five mile radius is saturated with Civil War history.

Before undertaking the new venture, Brother Martin and Brother McClure drove to Atlanta to counsel with Elder R.I. Keate, president of the Georgia-Cumberland Conference. They also discussed their plans with Elder J.K. Jones, then president of the Southern Union. They desired to work closely with the denominational leaders and organization.

The deal was closed. Wildwood Sanitarium and Hospital was born just a few weeks after the bombing of Pearl Harbor—in January of 1942. Dr. Hayward turned the property over to Wildwood's founders with only a $3,000 note of indebtedness.

"That's the most I've ever put my name to," Elder Frazee declared later as he signed the note. Elder Frazee, himself, had taken medical missionary training at Loma Linda.

The United States had declared war only a few weeks earlier, and all efforts and materials were being channeled toward the military build-up. Nonetheless, a group of workers came together at Wildwood to erect the new institution. The leaders and workers in this new venture began fulfilling their vision through prayer and an unshakable trust in God. Money came in to supply their needs for building materials and supplies. In answer to prayer, hard-to-get materials were found. Money came in from the most unlikely sources just in time to help continue the building. Finally, in 1944, the original sanitarium was completed.

> The purpose of Wildwood is to help harness some of the talents of people and to find an efficient way of using it for the furtherance of the cause of the Third Angel's Message.
>
> Every area of the work at Wildwood emphasizes the fact that this is a training institution. Basically, the student is taught three things:
>
> The first is to know God; to have a personal and deep experience with Him; to understand what He requires of His people before they are prepared to give the Loud Cry; and to be able to carry out these reforms.
>
> The second is how to share one's faith and to successfully witness for Christ. Every student is given the opportunity to be actively engaged in evangelism: door-to-door work, Bible studies, five-day plans, school temperance programs, cooking schools, breadmaking classes, weight-control programs, and other tools that we can think of to reach the hearts of people.
>
> The third is a means of self-support. This means learning to grow his own food, to maintain his car, to build his house, and to make a living, along with learning the art of cooking, child care, child guidance, etc.[1]

The influence on the laymen of the Seventh-day Adventist church of the self-supporting ministry begun at Madison College continued to be felt at Wildwood. During its early decades, the work at Wildwood expanded, and more leaders were needed with a vision of what God could do.

Warren Wilson came into leadership at Wildwood in the early 1970s, and he felt that small groups should spread throughout the country and even internationally. He began to talk and write about this.

One day someone called to offer Wildwood control of a vast farm in Zambia, Africa. As Warren recalled later, this offer left him speechless as he thought of the great distance between Zambia and Wildwood. When Warren had thought of expanding the work of Wildwood, he'd had in mind that perhaps "internationally" might include, say, the Caribbean and Central America.

The Wildwood influence has now spread throughout the United States, and it can be seen in such other schools as Stonecave, located in Sequatche Valley, Tennessee, (1958); Eden Valley Institute, Colorado, (1962); Beautiful Valley, Spencer, West Virginia, (1966); Castle Valley, Utah, (1970); Uchee Pines Institute, Seale, Alabama, (1970); Refugio Las Palmas, Honduras (1971); Catskill Missionary Outpost, New York, (1972); Shawnee Hills, southern Illinois, (1972); Riverside Farm Institute, Zambia, (1973); Silver Hills, British Columbia, Canada, (1973); Meadowbrook, Mountain Grove, Missouri, (1973); and Woodland Park, Ontario, Canada, (1974).

As of this writing, the directory of OCI lists 108 institutions, including fourteen Country Life vegetarian restaurants in thirty countries.

In 1983, Outpost Centers, Inc. was incorporated as a nonprofit corporation in the state of Tennessee. Warren resigned as president of Wildwood to give full time leadership to the worldwide work of OCI. He continued this work until a few months before his death in May 1989. Many of us who worked closely with Warren have a deep respect for this humble man of God. He was a Christian gentleman who showed a kind spirit for God to all he met.

As noted earlier, Harold Lance, who served on the executive board of OCI, was chosen as the new president to replace Warren Wilson.

Harold says that OCI conducts a spiritual retreat each year for its group of international workers and its board members. A new leader training seminar is held concurrently with the retreat. Divine guidance and good leadership are the keys to successful projects, so classes cover all facets of Christian administration (from spiritual principles to personnel counseling, and from financial concepts to agriculture).

Students from all major OCI adult training programs come to the headquarters in Dunlap, Tennessee for these two weeks of intensive study. They communicate with experienced leaders and enjoy both practical labor and hands-on application of classroom concepts. In past sessions, OCI has hosted over 100 guests, with fifteen to twenty countries represented.

The vision of educating students in practical methods of outreach that originated at Madison College is still very much alive. Training students to be self-supporting in their endeavors and to share the gospel of Jesus Christ is most important. OCI and its affiliated institutions demonstrate the ASI spirit of self-sacrifice as they carry their message and work to the world.

Note:

1. Wildwood Missionary Institute newsletter, September 1973.

14

The Roots of the Laymen's Foundation

The real story of the "widening sphere of Madison's influence" began with Mrs. Lida Funk Scott. Her father was the founder of the Funk and Wagnalls Publishing Company.

Mrs. Scott, through the providences of God, found herself in the Battle Creek Sanitarium. In the *Madison Survey*, she described her stay:

> In the year 1889, while I was a patient . . . I was seeking light on Bible topics. I studied eagerly everything . . . on the second coming . . . and on the other prophecies, and as a result I took a definite stand for the principles held by Seventh-day Adventists.[1]

Mrs. Scott was inspired by the Madison plan and determined to spread its mission. She dedicated herself to education and medical missionary work, providing schools, nursing homes, sanitariums, hospitals, and training facilities for nurses, teachers, and agriculturists. Many of the young people who attended these centers joined the ranks of Madison graduates in filling positions as gospel workers, both in the United States and overseas.

Mrs. Scott bought seventy-two acres in June 1921 and presented them to the board of managers. She funded the new sanitarium kitchen in May 1922. In October of that same year, she donated the Helen Funk Assembly Hall to Madison. In all, she gave thousands of dollars to help found the many small self-supporting units scattered throughout the southeastern states.

The first cafeteria and treatment room combination was started in Nashville in 1917. By 1920 its success led to a boom in that avenue of outreach. That year alone, cafeterias were started in Birmingham, Louisville, Knoxville, Memphis, and Chattanooga. So successful were these ventures that Madison began offering a short course of training for this type of work.

One of Madison's initial goals was to train workers quickly so that they might go out and start other self-supporting units. These units began appearing soon after Madison was established and continued to flourish throughout its history. Speaking of them, Dr. Sutherland said:

> One school built up a profitable lumber business, and in the school shop the boys and men were taught to make furniture . . . The activities of the school were reflected in the community in better houses, [and] new roofs . . . Another school established the only hospital in the community. Another town, whose only money crop had been tobacco, began to grow potatoes, alfalfa and fruit as a result of the school.[2]

A Medical Missionary Band was organized on June 21, 1919. This was probably a precursor of the Medical Missionary Volunteers (MMV). Its mission was to start new cafeterias, treatment rooms, sanitariums, and other types of rural outreach such as Madison had always undertaken. The time had arrived for this work to be organized.

Mrs. Lida Scott was the mainstay of this organization.

The MMV had a revolving fund from which to loan money for equipment to start new centers. In time this money was returned to MMV to be used again in opening other centers, then still others. Thus, they reasoned, a hundred dollars used in this way was equivalent to many hundreds of dollars given outright.

The Laymen's Foundation was incorporated in January 1924. It had essentially the same mission as the MMV—that is, assisting in the establishment of self-supporting enterprises in the South. The amount of money donated by Mrs. Scott eventually totaled approximately one million dollars. But she did more than provide money; she was actively involved until her death in 1945. She took a personal interest in the work.

The spirit of Madison College lives on in many of today's self-supporting institutions. Madison's original educational plan was to train students in applying practical principles to everyday life and to carry forward effective missionary work in their neighborhoods. The leaders and faculties of today's self-supporting institutions continue cheerfully implementing that original spirit of Madison.

Several schools and health institutions still operate under the Laymen's Foundation. These include: Fletcher School, Fletcher, North Carolina, founded by Professor and Mrs. Sidney Brownsberger in 1909; Chestnut Hill Farm, Portland, Tennessee, founded by Harriet Whiney Walen in 1908; Little Creek Sanitarium and Academy, Knoxville, Tennessee, founded by Elder and Mrs. Leland Straw in 1940; Laurelbrook Sanitarium and School, Dayton, Tennessee, founded by Mr. and Mrs. Robert Zollinger in 1953; and Harbert Hills Academy, Savannah, Tennessee, founded in 1951 by William E. Patterson. Mr. Perry Harbert donated the property for Harbert Hills Academy.

The educational, health, and agricultural work of the Laymen's Foundation is alive and thriving and continues reflecting the spirit of Madison College. Through the years, it has been an inspiration to hear testimonies detailing God's providences in these "units," rooted in the revelations of God to Ellen G. White and the desire of Drs. E.A. Sutherland and Percy T. Magan to train workers for service.

Notes:

1. *Madison Survey*, Nov. 10, 1920.
2. *Madison Survey*, Apr. 20, 1921.

15

A City of Refuge: La Vida Mission

La Vida (the Life) Mission! Truly, this mission is aptly named, for its loving ministry has brought life and hope, healing and Christian education to hundreds of isolated Navajo families.

The story of La Vida begins with Lily Nakai Neil. At age eighteen, she became the first baptized convert of Pastor Orno Follett, a Seventh-day Adventist missionary at Lake Grove Mission, New Mexico. The burden of Lily Neil's heart was to evangelize her own people. Lily and her devoted husband—a white trader—decided that Christian education was the key to reaching her Navajo people.

Lily had been one of the fortunate few. Even her limited education placed her high above the average Navajo woman of her day. With her keen mind and native abilities, she soon found herself in a position of honor and responsibility in the tribe. When a vacancy occurred in the highest governing body of her people,

Lily was elected as the first woman ever to sit on the powerful Navajo Council.

One night, as this Christian wife and mother pondered ways of bettering her people, she had a dream. "I saw a big circle of light," she explained, her amber face still radiant with the wonder of what she had seen. "Jesus was in the circle, in lovely shining garments. As I gazed at Him in adoration, He turned and smiled at me! While I still stood and watched in fascination, I became aware of footsteps—soft, moccasined footsteps, many hundreds of them—marching endlessly by. But they were outside in darkness just beyond the circle of light. Then the scene gradually changed. I saw more moccasined feet, but they were young, dancing ones. And many paused, turned, and came into the circle of light, and Jesus gladly welcomed them in.

"I understand from the dream that these moccasined feet represented my people and that the old ones, trudging by in the darkness of superstition and ignorance, would not respond so readily to the gospel. But the children and youth—these are the real hope of my people. I must do everything in my power to help them."

Lily never forgot her dream, but more than a decade would pass before the first pinpoint of light would appear, in the remote Tsaya area—fifty miles south of Farmington, New Mexico. As if in answer to her prayers, this first glimmer of light was a school—a Christian school—which boasted only a scant half dozen shy Navajo boys and girls. But the pinpoint of light grew.

The idea for a mission in the Tsaya area was first considered in 1948 and 1949. Soon after, several laymen began searching for land for the mission. In the early 1950s the first camp meeting and Vacation Bible School were conducted, and in 1960, land was purchased. Within two weeks electric service was installed. In 1961 an airstrip was built for people who wished to fly in and help with the school. A year later, the first class was held at the mission in its only building—a rock and pole-beam structure that had formerly been a trading-post.

Today Lily's "circle of light" has grown from a solitary missionary family in 1962 to a competent staff of twenty-four who work in ever-expanding posts of responsibility at La Vida Mission. The campus consists of 180 acres on which are situated a church, office, school, gym, medical clinic, dormitories, cafeteria, dorcas building, maintenance facility, eleven staff houses, a barn, and six greenhouses.

Gary Kaufman, current director of the Mission, reports that in 1991, young people from the ASI Youth Project constructed a duplex for staff housing. As of 1992, La Vida's playgrounds rang with the laughter of seventy-two students, ranging in age from four to fifteen. The school offers classes for preschool through the eighth grade. The original school building, which had three classrooms, has recently been expanded to include an additional classroom, art and music rooms, and a library. The dormitories house the students for eleven days of schooling. Then they spend three days at home before returning for another two-weeks of classes.

La Vida graduates are encouraged to attend Holbrook Indian School in Arizona, or an academy of their choice, where they continue to receive special attention by caring Seventh-day Adventists. As I write, one of the graduates is attending Campion Academy; one is at Sandia View Academy in Corrales, New Mexico; three are at Castle Valley in Utah; seven are at Holbrook Indian School, Arizona; and one is in San Juan SDA school in Farmington, New Mexico. All of these academy students are sponsored by La Vida Mission. Education is an opening wedge, just as Lily Neil knew it would be.

At first, the medical clinic at La Vida was located outdoors. In 1964, the clinic was operated from an old trailer. Now an attractive clinic building serves the community well. A registered nurse on the campus cares for the medical needs of the students and community throughout the week. Physicians and dentists take turns flying in each Wednesday for a weekly clinic session. Each year, medical and dental students from Loma Linda University come to help La Vida in caring for the health needs of the Indian children.

Education and health care are necessary and wonderful. But I observed something else wonderful as I visited the Mission. The children at the Mission school are very warm and receptive to caucasians who visit the school. They came up and talked with us and were very receptive to any kindnesses we showed them. As we stopped in the city of Farmington for lunch, it was a different story. We did not see this same friendly spirit in the Native American children we met there. The staff and students of La Vida Mission are making a difference in this needy world and are showing the spirit of ASI on the reservation!

16

What's Little Debbie Up to Now?

In 1934, a lively red-haired gentleman named O.D. McKee used his new panel truck as collateral for a $288 loan on a cookie shop. He wanted to compete with the snack wagons which catered to industrial workers in those days.

Early in 1935, he began to experiment with the hard oatmeal cookie his little shop was baking at the time. He made formula changes to make the cookie soft. He put two of his soft oatmeal cookies together with a fluffy filling in between. These "creme pies" sold for a nickel.

Mr. McKee was always looking for better ways to make his products, and he expanded his company time after time. Once he had to fill in for an absent employee. All day, he turned a hand crank. Later, he drove to a salvage yard and found a gear from an old washing machine. He went back to the bakery, replaced the hand crank, added a small motor, and began the automation process which turned his small bakery into one of the largest producers of snack cakes and wafers in the nation.

"The Oatmeal Creme Pie has been our mainstay," says Mr. McKee with a twinkle in his eye. It's still a favorite and as good a value today as it was fifty years ago.

> McKee Bakery in Collegedale, Tennessee, is a good example of ASI versatility in service. The bakery—"the home of Little Debbie" products—employs college students. Helping these students get a Christian education is an important part of their ministry. Their blessings are multiplied when these students graduate and go out into the field to witness for the Lord. The success that God has given McKee Bakery has enabled them to further the work through financial support. They have helped build over twenty-six churches.[1]

McKee Foods Corporation has also been very liberal in assisting many self-supporting institutions that are members of ASI. As I talked recently with Ellsworth McKee, president of McKee Food Corporation, he told me, "Although we have done well in our business, we have had some years that were not that good. But when the Collegedale SDA church was built, we gave more to that building fund than was deductible. Since then God has blessed us with wonderful success."

Another happy member showing the ASI spirit!

Note:

1. Robert H. Pierson, *Miracles Happen Every Day*, p. 68.

17

Miracles, Miracles, Miracles!

Danny Shelton and his family were active in a singing ministry for several years. They traveled to various churches and television stations with their gospel concerts. The theology Danny heard at some of those places greatly bothered him. Being a Seventh-day Adventist, he wondered how the clear, biblical truth could be aired throughout the world.

During the night of November 14, 1984, he received a strong impression that God was calling him to build a television station that could be used to televise the undiluted three angels' messages of Revelation 14. Here was a man in the building trade who sang gospel music wherever he was invited. He had no training in television broadcasting. Danny knew virtually nothing about TV production skills. Nonetheless, he was under strong conviction that God wanted him to begin this ministry.

As Danny thought during the night about the idea of an Adventist television station, he reviewed the lives of Bible characters such as Daniel, Moses, and Joseph, who accomplished great things for God. He thought about Ellen White and how God had called her—a young lady with physical problems and little education. All of these had overcome great obstacles to accomplish God's will. So Danny promised God that he would move forward to build this television station if He would supply the financial needs.

About 2 a.m., Danny called some friends in Louisiana and told them that God wanted him to build a television station. This family told him that they would like to come up and spend a couple of days with him. As they talked about the "dream," they went to see a charismatic pastor who had an existing television ministry with $100,000 worth of equipment. A man from Indiana had already come to see this pastor about purchasing all of his equipment. However, the pastor did not want to sell.

Danny told him that God wanted him to proclaim the three angels' messages around the world. But the minister believed that God had helped him obtain the equipment and felt that he should not sell. He was also reluctant to just give it away.

Danny was so seized with what God wanted him to do that he was unable to sleep that night. About 11 o'clock in the evening, Danny decided he should phone the pastor. He told Danny that all during the day he had been impressed to donate his equipment for the new station. He also said he was impressed that God was opening the way for southern Illinois to be a center for televising the gospel.

Danny went to California for a week to do some singing, and when he came back, he and his brothers went to Marion, Illinois, to visit a Christian television station. He had earlier met Clarence Larson, the engineer of the station, and knew him on a casual basis. Danny's purpose on this visit was to find out something about what it took to equip a television station.

After Larson had shown them through the studio, he said to Danny and his brothers, "Let's go to another room where we can talk." There, Larson said, "I have something I want to share with you. I have been impressed to tell you about installing an uplink. I could see that you didn't understand what an uplink was. So I asked you how far you wanted your station to broadcast, and you said around the world. And I said, yes, you can transmit around the world with this, but I had no idea what it's true purpose was to be."

Clarence then told Danny about the use of microwave technology and about microwave interference from telephone companies. He had been doing some studies about where a good place might be to install a microwave dish.

In about a week Danny shared with those in attendance at prayer meeting his vision of building a television station. They had special prayer about this new project for the Lord. A lady by the name of Fonda Summers, who had been attending the Revelation Seminar at the church, went home and thought about what she could do, as she wanted to do something for the Lord. But what could she do?

She felt she didn't have any special talent or anything to give. But she remembered how Moses had responded when the Lord wanted him to lead Israel. She also remembered that Danny had said he needed only two acres on which to build the station. She had two acres at the rear of her property that she was willing to give for this project.

Comsearch—a company located in Virginia—was retained to begin the expensive and extensive research necessary to be sure that this location would be acceptable for an uplink. After months of testing, Comsearch determined that this was the only part of Fonda's property that was free from any microwaves. It could not have been on the front or the middle part of her place, but the back two acres tested perfectly.

Then Scientific Atlanta from Indianapolis came and examined the location to be sure it would work for installing the dish. They said it would take $300,000 for the installation—and that they needed some money down, a letter of credit, and Danny's ability to make the payments as the construction progressed. Danny told them he had only $10,000 in the bank, but he wanted them to begin installation as soon as possible. The miracle of it all was in how God impressed people to send in money just as the payments were due. Still working with Clarence Larson, they applied for their license and received their approval.

With everything progressing well for the station, Danny decided they should build a 16,000-square-foot building to house their operation. This was September 1985, and at this point they did not have money for the building.

But first they had to build a road back to the building site. They rented a bulldozer to prepare the road. Danny contacted a company to purchase the gravel for the road and found it would be $6,000. They didn't have the money for it, but Danny knew God was leading and that He would provide. So he ordered the gravel. By the time it was delivered, he had received two letters. They both arrived the same day, and this was the only mail he received. The first was from a lady in Chicago who sent a check for $2,000. The second letter contained a check for $6,000—exactly the amount needed.

It was time to begin construction. On a Sunday, they were laying out the site for the building, still not knowing exactly how much it would cost. They knelt and prayed that God would lead in their needs. Danny went home, and his wife told him that a couple from Chattanooga, Tennessee, had called and said they wanted to come by to see the project. Danny phoned them and invited them to come up to see for themselves what was being done.

The Tennessee couple came and stayed for what turned out to be a week. Danny was not sure what they wanted to do. They didn't impress him as people who had financial resources. Every day they would watch as the digging progressed for the footings.

"Do you have the money for the concrete?" the husband asked.

"We have only two hundred dollars in the bank," Danny replied, "but if we don't spend it, why should we ask God to give us any more?"

"Do you mind if we watch you work? What are you going to do if it rains and fills up your ditches?" the visitor mused.

"I guess we'll have a river," Danny answered, "but that is not my concern. We are getting ready to build. We are going to go forward, spend what we have, and God will supply our needs."

The last evening of their stay, the guests wanted to talk with Danny and his group. They gave them a check for $25,000, and the next day presented them with another check for $25,000. This was exactly what was needed to begin building. Later, these people who had given $50,000 said that within a few weeks they had another $50,000 in the bank. They could not out-give the Lord!

As all this was happening, Clarence phoned one night to say he was concerned about the three-phase electrical supply needed to run the transmitting equipment.

"You know," he said, "your site is about a mile and a half from the main road, and there are no businesses out there that require this kind of electrical supply."

Clarence was so concerned about this problem that he wanted them to go out that evening to check the electric line. They drove down the road, shining their spotlight, looking for evidence of three-phase service. They could not find what they were looking for in the darkness. But as they came to the road leading to their property, Clarence gasped—the spotlight clearly showed three-phase electric service. The electric company said they had no idea why three-phase service had been extended out that far.

Within days of this experience, Danny and Linda were invited to attend the 1985 ASI national convention at Big Sky Lodge in Montana. Several ASI members had heard a little about Danny's project and wanted him to speak at the convention. Programs are planned months ahead, and the agenda was full. Friday afternoon was left open for the people to do what they wanted to do. When Friday afternoon came, it was pouring rain. This was the only time available for Danny to tell about his dream.

In the meantime, Danny's brother phoned to say that they were ready to pour the footings for the building. The concrete would cost $10,000—and they did not have $10,000. So after Danny had told his story, he went to a little table where Linda was selling their tapes. A man and his wife came by to purchase a couple of tapes and "paid" $10,000 by check for them to use in their work.

Returning home, they found that the building was proceeding well. The roof was on, and it was time to put in the electrical wiring. Danny's brother was an electrician, but he told Danny that he didn't feel he had the necessary experience to tackle the installation for a commercial building. They still did not have money to pay for the electrical work. So they all prayed again at the building site that God would provide.

Danny went home, and as he opened the door, the phone was ringing. He picked up the phone, and the caller told Danny he had just read the group's little newsletter and that he wanted to come down from Chicago to do their wiring. Brother Gonzalo Santos was a new Christian, and he wanted to do something for the Lord. During their conversation, Brother Santos told Danny he had done the electrical work for two other TV microwave installations.

Brother Santos brought a friend with him, and each weekend they drove down from Chicago and worked after sundown Sabbath and on Sunday to complete the electrical work. This multi-talented electrical engineer and his assistant would not accept a cent for their expert services.

Many miracles later, Three Angels Broadcasting Network sent its first programs to satellite just two years after Danny's impression from the Lord . . . to the surprise of many professionals in the communication field. Even the experts declare that satellite communication networks normally take three to five years to develop. Within 30 months of the initial vision, 3-ABN was producing many hours of Christ-centered programs in its own fully-equipped production studio and was sending SDA programming to satellite 24 hours a day! Praise God!

Three Angels Broadcasting Network is the first and only satellite network carrying 24-hour-a-day Christ-centered Seventh-day Adventist programming. This programming is sent 22,300 miles into space to satellite S4, transponder 9 and it is returned to earth and potentially received in the areas of North and Central America through UHF and cable stations; also hospitals, institutions, prisons, retirement centers and homes through receiving dishes. 3-ABN is not only received by 5-7 million home satellite dish owners in the United States, but through our cable outlets alone it can potentially reach over one million people. These outlets are growing at a rapid pace! 3-ABN has the unlimited potential to stretch the reach of the gospel AROUND THE WORLD by linking to international satellites.

At the present time there are operating stations broadcasting in Salem, and Johnston City, IL; Walla Walla, Yakima, and Seattle, WA; Grants Pass, Rogue River, Medford, Bend, and Klamath Falls, OR; Redding, and Palm Springs, CA; Campe Verde, AZ; Berrien Springs, and Grand Rapids, MI; San Juan, and Mayaguez, Puerto Rico; Minocqua, and Green Bay, WI; and Bozeman, MT. There are 21 other downlink stations that have construction permits for building in the United States; plus plans to build a station in Brazil. There is a state of the art Production Center already built in Romania with plans progressing in building a downlink station to cover Bucharest. In Nizhney Novgorod, Russia, an evangelism center has been purchased with a production center and our first Russian television station is now under construction.[1]

Notes:

1. From a report on the eighth anniversay of 3ABN in *3ABN, Catch the Vision*, 1992.

18

Harding Hospital: Seventy-Five Years of Ministry

The spirit of Harding Hospital (Worthington, Ohio)—a charter ASI member for over forty-five years—is impossible to understand without taking into account the firm religious foundation upon which it was built. A strong faith motivated the hospital's founder, Dr. George Harding II, as he envisioned a place where troubled people with mental and emotional problems could find help. Dr. Harding and his associates were dedicated Seventh-day Adventists who were deeply involved in the work of the church. That same faith has brought the hospital through many difficult times.

Early Days

First known as the Columbus Rural Rest Home, Harding Hospital began as a self-supporting medical mission. Although not owned or operated by the Seventh-day Adventist church, the hospital and the church were closely associated.

Dr. Harding was a long-time friend of Dr. E.A. Sutherland, and he had followed closely the development of Madison. In 1915 when Ellen G. White died, Dr. Harding was appointed to take her place on the Madison Board of Trustees. Both this close connection with the Seventh-day Adventist church and the opportunity to pioneer as a self-supporting institution have been highly prized through the years.

In 1947, when ASI was founded, Harding Hospital became a charter member, and through the years, Harding people have repeatedly provided leadership to the organization.

As soon as the sanitarium was established in Worthington, Ohio, a Seventh-day Adventist church was organized by the workers. Staff and patients alike looked forward to the Sabbath services, evening programs, and the weekly "question box" meeting conducted by Dr. Fred Weber and Dr. George Harding II.

Inspired by the example of Dr. John Harvey Kellogg at the Battle Creek Sanitarium, the "question box" meeting was an opportunity for Dr. Harding and his associates, Dr. A.B. Olson and Dr. Weber, to answer people's questions—whether of a psychiatric, medical, or religious nature.

Church services were held on the hospital grounds in the old lodge parlor. Music was regularly provided by the family of Daniel K. Nicola, manager of the sanitarium at the time. Later, a church school was established for the children of workers and was located in the hospital building now known as Oakmont. The Griswold Christian Academy in Worthington is the direct descendant of that school.

Dr. George Harding III, who took over management of the hospital after his father's death in 1934, was like his father in his commitment to patients, in his common-sense management, and in his own religious dedication. Yet he had his own ideas and a different emphasis.

Whereas Dr. Harding II had enjoyed the spotlight of public appearance and actively participated in religious meetings—especially enjoying the weekly "question box" meetings—Dr. Harding III was somewhat less extroverted and less interested in public meetings. Dr. Harding III was always willing to talk about spiritual issues, but preferred to do this in the privacy of his office rather than in the "question box" setting. As a result, during Dr. George Harding III's leadership, public appearances were less frequent, and the "question box" quietly disappeared.

Though the subject of ministering to patients' needs was frequently discussed in staff meetings, there was decreased public discussion during Dr. Harding III's leadership. His approach to spiritual matters was supported by his co-medical director, Harrison S. Evans, who likewise had a strong religious commitment. An exceptional teacher and public speaker, Dr. Evans was also more inclined to deal with these issues in private. (Both doctors served in leadership positions at Loma Linda University—Dr. Harding as president from 1948-1951, and Dr. Evans as Dean of the School of Medicine from 1975-1986 and president of Medical Affairs from 1976-1986.)

In 1939 Dr. Harding and Dr. Evans were also instrumental in founding another ASI institution—Worthington Foods. James L. Hagle, Allan R. Buller, and Dale Twomley of Worthington Foods have all been active in ASI. Allan Buller served as ASI president from 1967 to 1973.

Transition and Expansion

With the construction of the Worthington Seventh-day Adventist church in 1951, the weekly religious services which had been held in the lodge parlor moved off campus to a new church home on Griswold Street. The new church was fully supported by the leadership of the hospital. James L. Hagle, the hospital administrator, was the chairman of the church's building committee. Everyone rejoiced in the fact that the church now had its own home with ample facilities for all who wished to worship.

However, the pastor who had served both the church and hospital was now located off campus in the new church building. Initially, it was not recognized how much the church had influenced the hospital when it had been located at the lodge. The pastor was now called upon less frequently by the hospital staff of other faiths. They no longer had the degree of informal contact with him that had been available prior to the church's move in 1951. The time had come to seek a full-time chaplain for the hospital.

When Chaplain Darrell Nicola returned in 1962 from serving at the Bangkok Sanitarium and Hospital in Thailand, he accepted the position of chaplain at Harding Hospital. The appointment of a chaplain gave renewed visibility to spiritual issues within the hospital. Chaplain Nicola's influence soon began to be felt, not only through weekend religious services, but through his development of Faith and Life Groups for patients, which he conducted along with Elizabeth Sterndale, the director of Nursing Services, and now Director of Women's Ministries for the North American Division. Chaplain Nicola also pioneered pastoral participation in clinical team meetings within the hospital.

Chaplains Ossie Heaton and Gordon Creighton continued this direction and brought their own unique interests and skills to the hospital.

The arrival of Chaplain George Gibbs in September of 1982, however, brought a new and broader emphasis to pastoral care. In planning for Chaplain Gibbs's arrival, it was envisioned that an expanded hospital ministry would include more than ministering to patient's spiritual needs through individual contact, groups, and weekend services. Such a ministry would also emphasize the exploration of spiritual concepts and issues important to those treating the mentally ill.

This emphasis was developed with the involvement of

Kenneth Schelske, pastor of the Worthington Seventh-day Adventist church at the time. It was intended that the hospital chaplain and church pastor would be mutually involved with both the church and hospital. Pastor Schelske's tragic accidental death a few months later resulted in a necessary change in these plans.

Nonetheless, efforts were made to make the chaplain more available to all staff members and to involve them in a dialogue that would facilitate spiritual as well professional growth.

By the time Chaplain Bill Collins was added to the Pastoral Care department in 1983, pastors in the community were encouraged to become more actively involved with their parishioners when they entered the hospital. Religious services to meet the needs of Catholic and Jewish patients were initiated. A monthly Religion and Psychiatry Seminar provided an interdisciplinary forum where the staff could discuss religious and psychodynamic concepts and explore ways in which religion and psychiatry could be integrated.

An important contribution to the church at large in recent decades has been the annual Institute on Mental Health for Seventh-day Adventist pastors, teachers, and conference officials. Initiated by psychiatrists Charles L. Anderson and L. Harold Caviness and pastoral counselor Charles E. Wittschiebe of the Seventh-day Adventist Theological Seminary, these annual institutes have provided instruction in mental health, skills in recognizing signs of trouble, and counseling techniques to more than 900 Seventh-day Adventist clergy. Since 1953 this institute has given pastors an additional way to understand and help their parishioners, as well as an opportunity to learn how to work with psychiatrists, psychologists, social workers, and nurses who share a common belief.

Another important contribution to the church has been in the area of psychiatric education. Dr. George Harding

II was the first Seventh-day Adventist physician to specialize in psychiatry. Education was an important part of the hospital's mission, and the training of people to care for mental patients was emphasized from the beginning.

The residency program in psychiatry at Harding Hospital was first developed in 1936 by Dr. Harding III and Dr. Harrison S. Evans. Most Seventh-day Adventist psychiatrists from 1936 to 1966 were educated at Harding Hospital. To date the hospital has provided residency training for more than 100 people, emphasizing the integration of psychiatry and spirituality.

All of these advancements gave greater visibility to spiritual issues both within and outside the hospital.

Changing Attitudes Within Psychiatry

Harding Hospital's recognition of spiritual concerns was somewhat ahead of its time in comparison to psychiatry's traditional approach to religion. During the late 1970s and early 1980s, increasing interest in spiritual issues was occurring on a national level—as evidenced by President Jimmy Carter's acknowledgment of his personal faith. During this time, psychiatry's increasing recognition of the importance of religion in people's lives led to the establishment of a committee on religion and psychiatry—a standing committee of the American Psychiatry Association. Psychiatrists began acknowledging the importance of religion, as Freud's original ideas began to be modified. As a result, a new appreciation for religious perspectives emerged within psychiatry.

As noted earlier, this integration of faith with psychiatric treatment is not new to Harding Hospital. Prior to psychiatry's recent new perspective on religion, the author of this book teamed for many years with psychologist Vernon Shafer to conduct a weekly Bible class for patients. Other Harding psychiatrists—Henry Andren, S.R. Thorward, Joyce McCaughan, Herndon Harding, Sr., Richard Griffin, Bill Brunie, and Denis Mee-Lee—have also been significantly concerned with both the religious and spiritual dimensions of treatment.

Reaping the Rewards

And what has been the response to this ministry? A dietary worker, following her baptism, spoke about the quiet and steady influence her Adventist co-workers had upon her.

"I noticed a big difference in the way my Christian friends handled their day-by-day lives: the way they acted under stress, the way they talked, and the things they liked to do for fun were different. As a mother with two children, I began to wonder how I wanted to live my life and how I wanted my kids to grow up, so I decided the best place to start would be the Bible."

Many other lives have changed through being in a Christian environment and having the opportunity of relating spiritual issues to thoughts and feelings.

Seventh-day Adventists hold that freedom of choice—given at creation—is basic to the sanctity of human life and is to be recognized, preserved, and valued in the work of health care. Any exploitation of or undue influence on patients during a time of emotional or physical suffering is thus carefully avoided at Harding.

The hospital's interest in and emphasis on spiritual values has encouraged many staff members to review their own spiritual journey. In a 1992 survey of hospital personnel (the majority of whom are not Seventh-day Adventists), 69 percent of the respondents agreed or strongly agreed with the following statement: "The religious affiliation of the hospital helps create a caring environment for patients and staff." Eighty-six percent agreed or strongly agreed that "the spiritual dimension of life is important in understanding and treating emotionally troubled people," and 89 percent agreed or strongly agreed that, "the emphasis on healthful living, such as a healthy diet, optimal exercise, avoidance of non-prescribed drugs, alcohol, and smoking" was important to the hospital's overall therapeutic environment.

Continuing Mission

An ongoing spiritual commitment has been explicit from Harding Hospital's beginning. This commitment has been reflected by the leadership and staff of the hospital, as well as by trends in society. Dr. Harding II was a product of the times that produced men like John Harvey Kellogg and Billy Sunday. Dr. Harding III had a different emphasis and sought to bring professional and scientific credibility to the hospital program.

Today the hospital's commitment to faith in the healing process is as strong as ever. Every day, Harding's chaplains continue to explore faith issues with patients and staff of all religious backgrounds. Some of this spiritual exploration takes place within several of the hospital's specialized treatment programs.

In the Harding Addiction Recovery program, for example, patients with drug and alcohol problems work on their spirituality as a crucial part of their recovery. In the Day Hospital program, patients work on integrating their value and beliefs into their day-to-day living.

It is the continual goal of Harding Hospital to touch people's souls, as well as their minds and bodies—to provide a healing ministry based on divine love, human care, and compassion. Every moment of the day, Harding Hospital staff members continue to make outstanding contributions of time and talent in a way that fulfills the hope of the hospital's founders.

In this respect, the words of my grandfather,[1] written in 1916, are as valid today as they were seventy-five years ago:

> Since God's leading is so manifest, His directing providences so clear, we feel that upon us has been laid additional responsibility, and we enter upon this larger sphere with humility of heart, praying that He will lead

us as in the past, and that we may all be teachable. Our earnest hope is that the Sanitarium may prove a haven for suffering humanity and that physical health and spiritual enlightenment may be found here by many.[2]

Notes:

1. This chapter was written by Dr. George T. Harding, IV, M.D., president of Harding Hospital. The author expresses appreciation to Dr. Harding for taking time from his heavy responsibilities to contribute to this book. General sources consulted in preparing this chapter include: George T. Harding, IV, M.D., "Harding Hospital: Seventy-Five Years of Ministry," *The Harding Journal of Religion and Psychiatry*, vol. 10, no. 1, 1991—and George Gibbs, M.Div., "A Summary Report of the Staff Survey Regarding Religion at Harding Hospital, 1992."
2. Columbia Union *Visitor*, August 7, 1919.

19

ASI: Planning for the Future

Ray Hamblin, current national ASI president, recently shared with me some of ASI's plans for the future. Among them are the following youth-oriented projects:

- Two test programs to help students in finding work to obtain a Christian education are being conducted in Colorado and Michigan.
- More youth outreach programs and volunteer projects with Maranatha Volunteers International are being planned.
- Building projects are being planned to take place just prior to the national conventions, and these too will involve our young people.

Since 1985, the youth have had a full program running concurrently with the adult agenda at the national convention. Beginning in 1991, the Thursday evening meeting featured our youth sharing their personal witnessing outreach experiences. In 1992, the audience was deeply touched by the testimonies of the youth as well as by a presentation of ASI Youth in Action.

As a result of this youth emphasis, more younger families are joining ASI. Anyone who has studied history has noticed that any significant and successful movement—whether religious or political—has captivated the imagination and cooperation of its youth. Study the early history of the Adventist church and its pioneers, and you will find young people playing an active role. ASI is making wise plans for its future.

Let me share with you now some of the exciting projects ASI youth have been involved in recently.

> A large group of young people from Little Creek and Laurelbrook Academies in Tennessee arrived at La Vida Mission, 50 miles Southwest of Farmington, NM on July 11 via bus. Other youth came to join in the beginning of the long-planned event. Robert Zollinger of Laurelbrook Academy was the director of this ASI mission project.
>
> The youth team worked along with the Maranatha Volunteers to build the duplex for staff workers. It was a wonderful experience to accomplish the construction of much-needed housing at La Vida.
>
> ASI youth also conducted a ten-day Vacation Bible School coordinated by Mrs. Andrew (Shirley) Chastain of Ooltewah, Tennessee. Over 150 children were bused in by the La Vida staff, to attend the VBS.
>
> The mission project concluded with the youth going to Denver on July 31 to attend the National ASI Convention. Thursday evening the young people gave a presentation of the La Vida Mission project.[1]

★★★★

On a bone-dry hill on the western perimeter of a Mexican border town 30 miles east of Tijuana, 25 young

Americans spread out their construction equipment and went to work in the hot morning sun.

The concrete slab on which they were to build three school classrooms had been completed in previous weeks by other volunteer workers from America.

Within six days the new addition to the existing school would be enclosed and plastered, the roof on and all electrical service and insulation installed. It was a gift to the Adventist members of Tecate where the Baja California Mexican Conference headquarters is located.

But who were these people who so generously gave of their time and money to make it possible?

Earlier this year the leaders of Adventist-Laymen's Services and Industries (ASI) announced that they would co-sponsor this volunteer youth project with Maranatha Volunteers International and Friendship Missions, both ASI member organizations located in the Pacific Union Conference.

On July 26 they arrived. Nine ASI recruits came from as far away as South Carolina and Michigan. They were joined by 11 youth and adults from Weimar Institute who were headed by the project coordinator, Steve Brownell, Weimar boy's dean, and a contingent from the Roseville, California church, headed by Laurence Burn, youth pastor. Under the supervision of Jim Genn, Hughson, California, soon the walls were up and the roof was going on the 20' x 80' structure.

The addition will allow the school's present enrollment of 75 to increase to 130. Because of high demand for the fine quality of Adventist education, the school will be immediately filled, said Dale McBride, ASI's liaison who lives in nearby El Cajon, California.

While most of the workers were busy with construction, a small team conducted a daily Vacation Bible School program. Brownell's wife, Frankie, VBS coordinator, said 33 children came the first day. Soon they had

50 students joining in the classes, recreation and refreshments.

"The Adventist message is going like wildfire in Mexico," McBride said. "There are 60 new congregations in northwestern Mexico, and they all need churches. But the people are too poor to build them. That's where we fit in."

ASI provided $25,000 for building supplies for this project, one of their 1992 projects funding programs.[2]

Notes:

1. *Navajo News*, September 1991.
2. C. Elwyn Platner, Pacific Union *Recorder*, September 7, 1992.

20

We Welcome You!

The purpose of this book has been to acquaint readers with a dynamic organization for self-employed Seventh-day Adventist business and professional people. Adventist-Laymen's Services and Industries (ASI), now about 1,000 members strong, is dedicated to supporting and advancing the mission of the Adventist church.

ASI is not primarily a fund-raising organization. Instead, it was formed to encourage outreach activities within the church, community, and marketplace. The lay movement that began with Madison College continues to the present. ASI is a driving force for spiritual activities. For as long as I can remember, the laymen of ASI have voluntarily taken up offerings to help in outreach activities chosen by the organization. Neither the General Conference nor any other conference has urged any fund-raising programs.

The General Conference—as well as union and local conferences—enjoys a mutually pleasant relationship with

ASI. Some of the speakers at ASI conventions are leading church administrators. The loyal support of our ASI members to the denomination has provided a beautiful model of cooperative effort in the Lord's work.

This book is addressed to those Adventists who are busy in their corporations, companies, or medical practices—who are pushed to the limit with all kinds of demands and responsibilities. You may be so busy that you think you cannot even consider becoming a member of another organization. Around 1,000 ASI members are under the same pressures as you are, but they feel they cannot afford to miss one ASI convention. Why? Because there is something greatly refreshing and restful about coming apart from the rat race to fellowship with other brothers and sisters in the Adventist church.

The ASI spirit I have written about in this book is the secret to catching a vision of something beyond the often numbing routine of daily activity. I have personally observed many families who are living proof that something came alive for them as they attended an ASI convention. Hundreds are captivated by the testimonies of fellow lay members who share what they are doing in outreach. But more important than what they say is the spirit in which they say it. As these testimonies are shared, a large number in the audience say to themselves, "If they can do it, I can do it!"

At one of the ASI national conventions, a lady introduced herself to us as Madlyn Lewis-Hamblin. Her parents had been our neighbors years earlier at Emmanuel Missionary College. Madlyn and her husband Ray had come to the convention to see what this thing called ASI was all about. The Hamblins own and operate a printing company in Tecumseh, Michigan.

They were so moved by what they experienced that they went home much different people than when they had come to the convention. Ray told me later that they had concluded that business and religion did not go well together. However, they changed their minds because of what they had heard and experienced.

The Hamblins decided to place a literature rack in the lobby of their business, and to their amazement, the books disappeared at a rapid clip. They were surprised to find that their own employees were taking many of the books. After reading some of the literature, these employees began to ask questions. Within a few months, one of their men had received the Lord and became an Adventist. One day their accountant asked Ray why they gave so generously to the church. What an opportunity to witness! And witness they did! They studied with their accountant, and he was baptized!

Before long, the Hamblins attended a meeting to learn how to conduct Revelation Seminars. They went home from that meeting and began to plan for the first seminar. They mailed out invitations to the people of Tecumseh, Michigan. A good group of people came and completed all of the seminar. As a result, five people were baptized and joined the Adventist church.

This was the beginning of a lifestyle change for the Hamblins as they shared Christ in the marketplace—or any place! The ministry of the Hamblin family has grown and expanded. Since these Revelation Seminars began, a Seventh-day Adventist church has been organized and a lovely new sanctuary built in Tecumseh, Michigan. All of this outreach began at an ASI national convention!

ASI seems to choose officers who give leadership in business and evangelistic outreach. In 1989, Ray Hamblin was elected president of the national ASI. Under his leadership, the organization is making great strides both in membership growth and in the outreach activities.

You are invited, my reading friend, to attend an ASI national convention—or your union chapter convention—at the very next opportunity. Discover for yourself the fellowship and the spirit that permeates the organization, and decide if you think an association with ASI would benefit you and your family and your business.

The stated objectives of ASI are:

1. To encourage and promote the development of privately owned businesses and enterprises operated by Seventh-day Adventist laymen throughout the world field.

2. To encourage Seventh-day Adventist church members in privately owned enterprises of various types to unite their efforts with those of the denominationally operated enterprises in the furtherance and extension of the gospel in their immediate communities, and to the ends of the earth, according to their abilities and opportunities.

3. To encourage the owners of such enterprises to commit themselves to work in full and complete harmony with the standards and objectives of the denomination in their relationship with conference and church administrations, ministers, church members, and the people of their communities.

4. To provide a means by which members of the Association can become more effective in their work through exchange of information, coordination of objectives and effort, and inspiration of Christian fellowship.

Those who wish to join ASI can obtain an application from the local conference ASI secretary. Full instructions are printed on the applications. Any additional questions you may have can be answered by the local ASI secretary, or you can contact the national ASI office at the General Conference of Seventh-day Adventists, 12501 Old Columbia Pike, Silver Spring, MD 20904. The direct phone number to that office is (301) 680-6450.

What is the ASI spirit? It is the complete dedication of each member to the personal ministry of sharing the very life and work of Jesus Christ in the marketplace.

We welcome you to the adventure of your life! And we challenge *you* to seize the ASI spirit!